Remembrances

OF KENYA

The Sotik Years

Heather,
May God bless you in your
future endeavors!

Laurie

SPIT A BLESSING

Remembrances of Kenya

THE
SOTIK
YEARS

Laurie Wall Bates

CreateSpace.com-a Division of Amazon.com

Spit A Blessing
Remembrances of Kenya

The Sotik Years

Copyright© 2010 by Laurie Wall Bates

Printed by CreateSpace.com—A Division of Amazon.com

ISBN 1449949932

EAN 13 9781449949938

Verses marked (TLB) are taken from The Living Bible, Copyright© 1971; (NIV) are from the New International Version, International Bible Society, 1984; (NLT) are from the New Living Translation, Tyndale House Foundation, 1996 All other quotations are duly noted.

Cover design by Lydia & Tony Di Cino, Tommy Wall and Laurie Wall Bates. All photos are used by the permission of and are the property of the Wall and the Bates families. Editing and creative input for this book was given by the Bates, Butcher, Di Cino, Wall and Walton Families. Thank you for answering endless questions.

— ·· — ·· —

"we're storytellers,
both of us.
I speak mine out;
you write yours down."

Movie: <u>Big Fish</u>

— ·· — ·· —

ACKNOWLEDGEMENTS

TO my family : My husband, Daryl, who was with me while these stories were 'written' and is there with me still while even more stories are continuing to unfold. Our children Lydia, Steven and Lee, whose questions about our life in Kenya brought about this book. Our newest additions; son-in-law, Tony and grandson, Gabriel, who have brought such joy into our home. (Tony, thank you for watching Gabriel and everything else you did so Lydia could cook, edit, type and everything else she did.)

TO my parents: My father, Tommy and my mother, Carrie, who are 'storytellers both'. Pop 'speaks his out' both old favorites and some new ones created right on the spot. Mama 'writes hers down' so family and friends can remember and have them always.

TO my siblings and their families: My three sisters, Carla, Davan and Teddie and my two brothers, Steve and Tim. Being near the middle, I always had someone to talk with, to do things with or to just hang around with. You were such a part of my imaginative, formative years and y'all continue to be there for me. I am grateful to be surrounded by such support and creativity.

TO my family on my husband's side: Daryl's parents, Bill and Evelyn whose years of service taught us to persevere. His three brothers, Lawrence, James and Bruce, who along with their families, have supported us in our efforts wherever we are and whatever they may be. It's comforting to be accepted just as you are.

AND DEDICATIONS

TO our American teammates: The Allison, Chowning, Kehl, Rogers, Van Rheenen and Vick families; along with the many other missionaries we worked with over the years. You are not my family by blood, but we have a bond that is so close, we can always pick up where we left off ... whether it's been days, months or years!

TO our supporters (churches and individuals): whose vision to send a family to Africa so the Kenyans could learn about God, made this entire experience possible.

TO our Kenyan brothers and sisters: who so humbly, quietly, patiently and usually, without even realizing it, taught me lessons about God and life that have been written on my heart.

And to the Almighty, all-knowing God: the greatest storyteller, who brought all of these 'stories' into my life.

Thank you to you all!! The pieces of you that I carry around with me in my heart have made me what I am today.

THANK YOU SO MUCH

Kongoi mising (Kalenjin)

Asante sana (Kiswahili)

CONTENTS

"Were you scared…?"
"Yes. Well, I don't know. Sometimes,… it was beautiful."
"I wish I could have been there with you."
"But you were!"
Movie: Forrest Gump

INTRODUCTION

"What's it like over there? Do you live in a mud hut? Were there lions in your backyard? What did you eat? Were you ever scared?" These are just a few of the questions usually asked of us whenever we returned to America from Kenya.

I've told our kids stories to help them untangle their memories of furlough times in America from their everyday lives in Kenya. (No, Lydia, there was not a McDonalds® in our little village of Sotik.) I've shared some experiences with family and friends about our life in Africa. And like most missionaries, I've pulled numerous examples from our life there as illustration. But how do you answer simple questions with the complex answers that are Africa?

Because of all these questions, I began toying with the idea of putting these memories down in black and white. I really felt convicted when I attended a lecture on writing where the speaker said, "Everyone has a story to tell; but if YOU don't tell it, who will?"

My mother, who has written several books said, "After three generations, no one remembers anything about you. I want our life to be remembered so, I'm writing about it."

I've always been intrigued by a good story in whatever form that it happens to take; book, movie, song, or even a picture. Stories have been used since the beginning of time as a means to remember an event or simply to communicate. There is an old saying that goes something like this: 'In order for something to be remembered it takes at least two people; one person to tell the story and the other person to listen to it.'

The words I am putting down on paper are just a few of our experiences while we were in Kenya. I didn't keep a diary while we lived there. I've kicked myself over and over for that. So I am writing from _my_ memories and point of view. (To those of you who were there with me when any of these things happened, I'm sorry if there are details I didn't get exactly right.) I was naïvely bold when we began our life in Africa. My husband Daryl and I, having been married for four years, were setting off on our African adventure at the ripe old age of twenty-six to make a difference in the world, not realizing what a difference this journey would make in our own lives.

Cross-cultural missions can either 'make you or break you.' It can be a time of hardship, loneliness and fear. But it can also be a time of discovery, joy and dependence on God and His sovereignty. In view of the fact that Kenya is a developing nation, I expected it to be 'behind' in many respects. But there were times I found Africans to be more advanced than Americans in certain situations. The gracious way they treated others and the way clocks did not rule over people are a couple of examples. Tasks were set aside; watches (when worn at all) were ignored for the chance to talk with a visitor. Tea or whatever food was available was brought out and shared in order to make you feel accepted and welcome; even if it meant the host would later have to go hungry.

Among the members of our team, I felt the least pre-pared for the journey on which we were about to embark. But I was soon to learn many lessons that I think I never would have learned any other way; lessons I still hold dear to my heart today. Even though some of our time in Kenya was not enjoyable or satisfying, it was so life altering for me that I would not trade it for anything. It was there that my faith in God truly became my own.

I look forward to sharing some of those experiences and life lessons that I learned with you. There is nothing miraculous in them; just the struggles of a young woman trying her best to fit into a culture that was not her own. I encourage you to put yourself into the stories. Think about how you would have reacted in the same situations. Hopefully, you'll take away a better understanding of yourself and God's sovereignty, like I was able to do.

I'm doing my part by telling the stories. I hope you
will do your part by 'listening' and then remembering.

SPIT A BLESSING

Remembrances of Kenya

THE
SOTIK
YEARS

Laurie Wall Bates

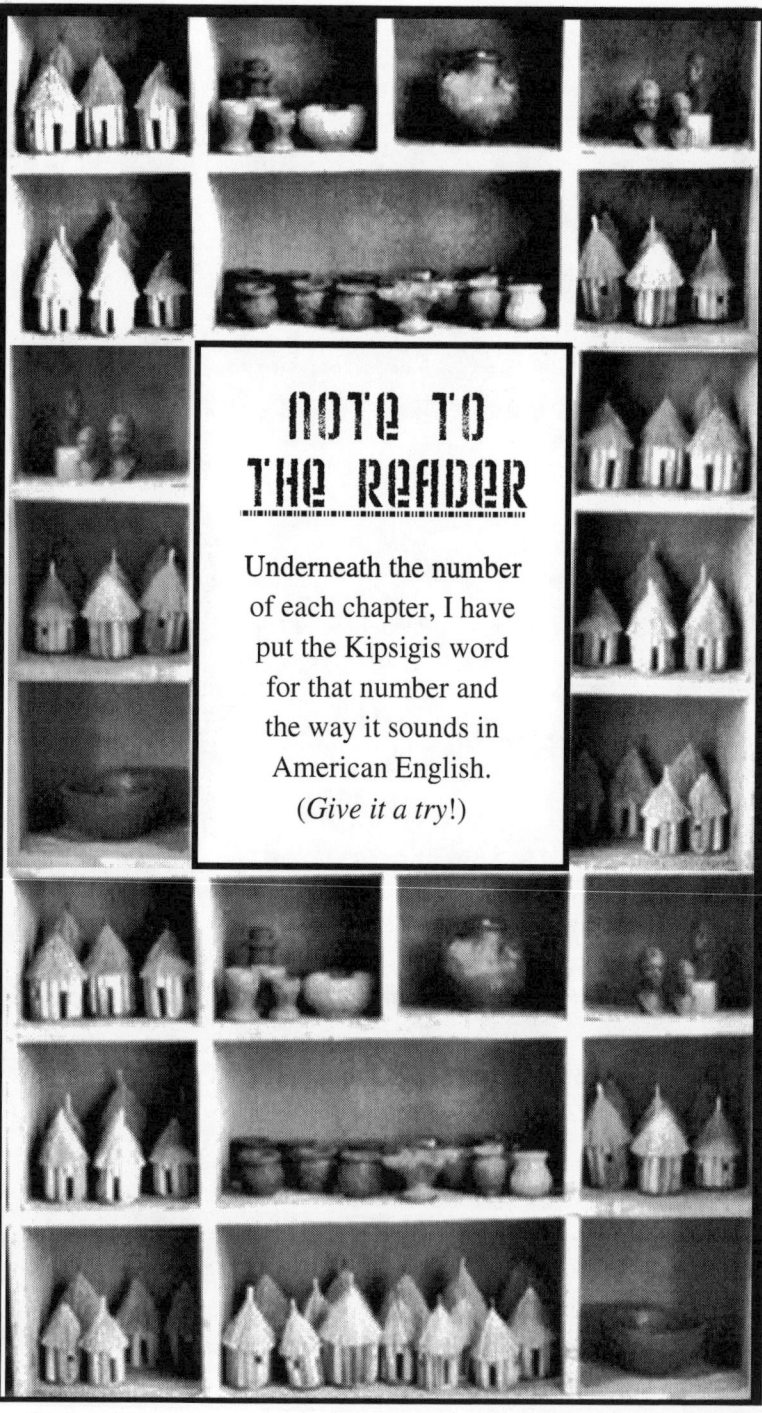

NOTE TO THE READER

Underneath the number
of each chapter, I have
put the Kipsigis word
for that number and
the way it sounds in
American English.
(*Give it a try!*)

ONE

agenge
(ah gehn geh)

"Could it be that He is only waiting there to see; if I will learn to love the dreams that He has dreamed for me?"
Song: I Will Listen by Twila Paris

LAUNDRY WITH A MISSION

How does someone decide to leave all they are familiar with and go to a foreign land to live and work in the midst of a people they don't really know? Well, in our case, it all began with a simple basket of laundry. My husband Daryl and I were married during the summer before our last year of college. He had one semester left to graduate and I had two. At that time in my life, I pretty much lived in the moment. All I could think about was getting my degree finished and adjusting to our new marriage. Daryl, however, thinking to the future, decided to stretch his studies out to two semesters so we could graduate at the same time. Doing that allowed him to work more and me less, which I appreciated since I had the heavier school load.

Before long, we learned to balance work, study and fun. We both belonged to social clubs before we were married and we continued to be involved with them afterwards. The clubs' various sport activities gave us an opportunity to blow off some steam from our studies and to develop friendships (many of which we still have to this day). One Saturday afternoon, a club mate of Daryl's named Eddie, called to say he was doing laundry in the Laundromat next to our apartment building. He wanted to know if he could drop by during the different cycles to talk to us about something. After setting a time for 'the talk', my inquisitive nature began wondering what it was that he wanted to talk to us *both* about.

By this time we had been married around nine months, while Eddie had been married a few weeks. Daryl thought he just wanted to talk over club matters. I, on the other hand, thinking they could have easily discussed that over the phone, decided he wanted some marital advice from us since we had been married so much longer! We were both wrong. Never could we have imagined the change that was to occur in our lives from that simple conversation.

After small talk was passed, Eddie began to explain, "Kathy and I are part of a group that is trying to find people interested in forming a team to do foreign missions. We were wondering if you might be interested in joining us. The team will probably be going to Africa."

"... A F R I C A ... "

The rest of the conversation was a blur to me. I just remember sitting there thinking, "*Not marital advice...Daryl and ME...living in Africa*?!" I shook myself out of the stupor I was in as Eddie stood up, grabbed his laundry basket, and said he needed to check on his clothes. After Eddie was out the door, we turned to each other with questioning looks on our faces and launched into a discussion. Daryl seemed interested at the prospect. I felt both shocked and intrigued at the same time. We were already committed to a six-week mission trip to Australia just days after our graduation, so the idea of missions was not totally foreign to us. But a six-week trip and actually moving to a foreign country to live and work were two very different things.

While I had been sitting there in my stunned state, Daryl had been listening. He told me Eddie's group had not formed a formal team yet. They were still in the meeting-together, getting-to-know-each-other and planning stage. At their last meeting, they had decided to try to enlarge their team. And what better place to do that than at the Christian University we were all attending? After they left that meeting, they were to pray and think about other people that could potentially become part of their team. That was how Eddie came to approach us.

We decided to go to a few of their meetings to get to know the others in the group and to get a better understanding of what their plans were. The more we met together, the more interested we became. And, the more underprepared I felt for the work that might possibly be before us. Everyone else, including Daryl, had degrees that would enhance a mission team—Bible, education, nursing, and counseling. But, what was my degree in? Fashion Merchandising! What possible use could that have on an African mission field? With our graduation and trip to Australia looming before us, we decided to focus our attentions more on those two things for the time being.

What a milestone our graduation day was. I was so thankful that Daryl had thought ahead so that we could share this moment. It was wonderful that within that sea of black caps and gowns, we were able to sit side-by-side holding hands as we met this next step in our lives together, Daryl Bates followed by Laurie Wall Bates.

Our time in Australia helped me to see that even though your surroundings may be unfamiliar, people are just people.

Daryl had gone on a summer campaign to Brazil as a freshman and already had some cross-cultural experience. After our time in Australia, I too had gleaned some knowledge which helped to allay some of my fears. Upon our return, we began meeting with the group again with renewed interest. After all, God calls all types of people to do missions, so why not me?

Harding University–Searcy, AR

As we continued to meet for the next year and a half, this question would arise, *"Where in the world* (literally) *should we go?"* At one meeting, we even handed out pieces of paper so we could write down the top three places we wanted to go. We did this in an attempt to try to narrow down the possibilities. Since five out of the now eight people in our group had been to Kenya on survey trips, it wasn't surprising that the predominant place written down was Africa. Survey trips are typically a three to six week period of time where you travel around a country doing research, if there are no missionaries there for you to garner information from. When there are missionaries in the country, they are a great resource and can serve as interpreters when interviewing local people. These surveys help you get a much better understanding of how you would live and work in that country and what your receptivity will most likely be like. And, most importantly, you find out if you are adaptable enough to handle the differences between your culture and theirs.

Africa is a huge continent with a diverse population and ethnicity. You can fit two of the contiguous United States across the top and one in the lower portion. After some dialogue about the different areas in Africa, someone stated that since so many of our group had already spent time and money in going to eastern Africa on survey trips, why not just concentrate our attentions there? We thought that was a great idea and it helped us to make a more informed decision. We left the meeting with three areas of East Africa to think about: the coastal region of Kenya on the Indian Ocean, the central area of Kenya around the city of Machakos (east of Nairobi) and a lake region in the country of Tanzania, located directly below Kenya. Before our next meeting in two months time, we were to commit those three areas to prayer to determine _the place_ we believed God was leading our group to. By that time, our team was made up of four couples. We were all in our twenties with only eighteen months difference between our ages.

During that time of prayer, each couple received a package in the mail from a team in Sotik, Kenya. The package consisted of a cassette tape, a video tape and a letter. In each of these formats, the Sotik team spoke of their church planting ministry in that area. They explained that time had come for them to begin the phasing-out process after years on the field. But they felt these churches still needed missionary input. They were inviting us to serve as a follow-up team to their work. The three families on the Sotik team were: Fielden & Janet Allison and their five children, Jeffrey, Katherine, Martha, Nicole and Chris; Richard & Cyndi Chowning and their three children, Heather, Aaron and Naomi; and Gailyn & Becky Van Rheenen and their four children, Jonathan, Deborah, David and Becca. Two of the three families were planning to accompany their children, who were now ready to start college, back to America. Most of their children had been born in Africa and _all_ had grown up there. They saw Kenya as home and America as foreign. Having their parents go back with them, to their foreign homeland of America, would help them to better adjust to the 'culture shock' that they were sure to have.

One month later, when our team got back together, we discussed the content of the tapes and letter and the timing of their arrival. We couldn't get over the fact that they came during the time we had dedicated to deciding where to work and live in East Africa. Most of our teammates knew these families well and had stayed with them during their survey trips. We all agreed to answer the call we felt God had sent to us through the delivery of those packages. Since the question of where to go was now settled, we needed to decide, "When?"

There was still so much yet to be put in place. (The need to find supporting congregations, develop relationships with them and to finish school.) We decided that eighteen months should be enough time to get it all accomplished. We then placed a call to the Sotik team when we knew the men would be together for their weekly planning session. In that call, we told them we were accepting their invitation to come and the target date we had set to be there. During that conversation, we found out the Van Rheenen family would already be back in the States by the time we moved there. But the other two families would still be there, so that there would be some overlap, a 'passing on of the baton', so that they could have some time to mentor us.

With these important decisions made, the new 'Sotik Team' (as we began thinking of ourselves), needed to decide something else; "*How long do we stay?*" We discussed what we thought our length of commitment should be. Over and over we heard our team throw around the idea of a ten to fifteen year commitment, which was a little unnerving to me. All sorts of doubts and questions began to run through my head. *Will I really be able to cope in Africa? Can I stand to be away from my family for that long? Is my faith strong enough to fully rely on God and go to a place I've never laid eyes on? What if I get there and I can't stand it? What if I can't last ten to fifteen years?* I finally decided to share these feelings with our team.

The New 'Sotik' Team (l to r): Eddie & Kathy Rogers, Susan & Kevin Kehl, Brenda and Dave Vick and Daryl & Laurie Bates

They understood all my doubts and came up with a couple of helpful suggestions. One was that we make a five-year commitment instead of one for ten years or more. After five years, if we wanted to extend our time, we could. Feeling that I could face anything for five years, it made me less anxious and like a huge weight had been lifted off of me. The second suggestion from our team was that we go on a survey trip to Sotik to take a look at it for ourselves. This seemed like a waste of money since we planned to move there in the near future. But they asked what would be the bigger waste of money: the cost of the trip, or the cost to ship our belongings there, buy a vehicle, set up house and THEN figure out that I couldn't handle it? With both of those suggestions, I felt a greater peace and we made the decision to take a survey trip.

Neither Daryl nor I were very good at fundraising. We sent out appeals to try to raise the $2000 needed for tickets and expenses, but after raising only a little over half of that, the amount seemed to hover there. We felt discouraged and decided to pray together before Daryl left for work. (After graduating from college, we moved to Memphis so Daryl could begin graduate work. I worked full-time as a Decorating Consultant at the local mall while Daryl attended school and worked the night shift at FedEx.) After our prayers, Daryl left earlier than usual to attend a work-related meeting. Feeling despondent, I decided to go to bed.

The next morning as I was getting ready, with Daryl the one that was sleeping, I saw a note on the dining room table from him that read, *'Great news at the meeting. We'll talk when you get home.'* I thought it must be some kind of bonus, so I just smiled and left for work.

When I got home, Daryl had unbelievable news! One of the perks of working with FedEx in those days was the "inter-airline" discounts they shared with other companies in the commercial travel industry. We had taken advantage of these many times over the years to meet with our team and to see Daryl's family who lived in Virginia. Daryl usually flew 'jumpseat' (in the cockpit with the flight crew), something that was offered free to all FedEx employees. I flew commercially at a deep discount. (After 9-11, this changed.)

The meeting of the night before was to inform the employees that since FedEx had recently gone international, the reciprocal airline discounts would also. After Daryl got off work that night, he checked into the price of tickets under the new agreement. He found out we could BOTH fly to Nairobi and back for $800!! That changed the $1200 we had raised from a deficit amount to a surplus amount. One of the conditions of the discount was that we had to fly standby, meaning that we could board if there was space available. If so, we flew; if not, we would have to wait for the next available flight. But even that God turned into a blessing. In Amsterdam, when the count seemed to take an extra long time, we nervously watched the agents checking and re-checking the plane's manifest. We thought for sure we would have to stay behind. Finally, the agent motioned for us to come up to the desk. She told us the plane was unusually full and they would have to bump us up to business class!

Exhilaration ran through us as we began our descent onto the runway of the Jomo Kenyatta International Airport in Nairobi. Looking out the window, I halfway expected us to land on a large grassy plain with 'savages' over to the side yelling and shaking their spears at us. Intellectually, I knew you shouldn't land a 747 onto a grassy field and that the Kenyans we were to meet wouldn't be dressed in that manner; but that didn't keep those old stereotype images from TV and movies from popping into my head! Instead, as we craned our necks to look out the window, we saw the typical patchwork of urban sprawl—roads, houses and buildings. Even though the view from above was typical, the view at ground level was not. There is nothing like landing on foreign soil and feeling completely out of your element yet excited with anticipation at the same time.

We'd done a lot of reading to prepare ourselves for the trip. We had learned that Kenya is about the size of Texas and has a very diverse topography. To the east are beautiful white beaches with swaying palm trees and the warm crystal clear aqua waters of the Indian Ocean. To the west is Lake Victoria, that big blue dot you can see on any map of Africa, and rain forests where beautiful black and white colobus monkeys swing in the trees beside all manner of exotic birds. To the north are wide stretches of desert where camels are used because of the scarcity of water. To the south are where many of the game parks are located because of the golden grassy plains of the savanna in the Great Rift Valley. In the area, where Nairobi is located, all of these elements converge to make an atmosphere which is close to paradise. It's no wonder Nairobi has the nickname, 'Green City in the Sun.'

As we made our way to passport control we got a chuckle out of the 'VISA' information sign. Someone had taken a cardboard advertisement for the VISA Credit Card, torn off the well known band of color above the word 'VISA' and drawn an arrow through the bar of color underneath the word to point the way to the visa checkpoint. On our way to collect our luggage, we noticed all the different nationalities represented around us. The most exotic were the ladies from India who were draped in brilliant colored saris, infused with gold and silver threads. The buzz of the different accents swirling around us helped me to understood more clearly what Dorothy meant in the Wizard of Oz when she said, "Toto, we're not in Kansas anymore."

When we were finally able to pass through the doors of the 'Arrivals Gate' into the brilliant tropical sunshine pushing its way into the airport, even the air had a different smell to it. Our new teammate and coworker, Richard Chowning, was there to pick us up. He immediately immersed us into this foreign culture by taking us to an East Indian restaurant for lunch. We told him we weren't very hungry, but the truth was we didn't see any food on the buffet line that we recognized or could even pronounce! Richard urged us to eat by saying it would be a while before we ate again. Carefully, we picked our way through the offerings and found some things to eat. It's funny how completely you can change your opinion on things once they become more familiar. We later learned to love East Indian foods and often get a craving for it.

We were seriously jet-lagged. After lunch I was hoping for a nap, but Richard assured us the best thing to do to get our 'body clock' on Kenya time was just to keep in motion until bedtime. We accompanied him on his errands, going from shop to shop as he worked off of a list he kept in his pocket. Richard spoke in English, Kiswahili and sometimes a blending of the two. We were very impressed, and I for one could not imagine myself ever doing such a thing.

As we trudged along trying to stay awake, I was overwhelmed by how crowded the streets and roads were. If the climate could be described as paradise, the traffic we encountered certainly could not. It was made up of people walking everywhere, donkeys pulling carts, buses and taxis. They were so laden with bundles, tied onto every surface; that they looked like they would topple over at any second. The buses and taxis were so crammed full of people, we could see them standing in the aisles and even hanging out the doorways. But such is the throng which is Nairobi. When we arrived for our survey trip in June of 1986, it was a city of three million souls; made up of skyscrapers, traffic jams, poverty and beauty.

LESSON LEARNED

God can use laundry, an airline agreement
or anything else of His choosing to
fulfill the plans (dreams) He has for you.

Nairobi Traffic—Notice location of steering
wheel, direction of oncoming traffic and
window stickers behind the rear view mirror

TWO

oeng
(oh ang)

"If you don't go after what you want, you'll never have it. If you don't ask, the answer is no. If you don't step forward; you're always in the same place."
Nora Roberts

DREAMS BECOME REALITY

'Hurry up and wait' is a big part of African living. Whenever we needed to stand around to 'wait' for assistance, to checkout, or to do whatever, I would ask Richard why he had chosen this store in particular or the item he was purchasing. After he would explain, I wrote down his answers in a steno writing tablet I had brought along to journal our trip experiences. (I had no idea how valuable all these little notes I was taking would later become.) AT LAST, Richard finished his shopping for the day and we were taken to the place where we were to sleep for the night. It was named The Ibis Hotel, after a graceful Egyptian bird that migrates to Kenya. The name was rather grand in comparison to the actual accommodations that were offered. The hotel room had cement floors and walls, two twin metal cots for us to sleep on and bars on the windows. The only thing that kept it from looking like a prison cell was the plain, faded bedcovers and their matching curtains hanging askew on either side of the barred windows. Even though the furnishings were a bit stark, the room was clean and quiet. I was so exhausted by this point I think a bed of nails would have looked inviting. Walking into the room, we put our bags on the floor beside the beds to deal with later.

I plopped down on the bed and kicked off my shoes with a grateful sigh. While we were relaxing, Richard came in to discuss supper plans. I told him I was too tired to eat. Even if it was only 7:00 p.m. by our watches, my 'body clock' said it was 3:00 a.m. and time for bed. Looking over at Daryl who I knew was hungry; I told him he was welcome to leave me behind and go out to eat with Richard. Daryl could tell I was beyond tired, so he decided to stay behind with me. He made a simple meal with some food items we had brought along with us. As we got ready for bed, we talked about the different things we had noticed throughout the day. I wrote a few more things down in my journal and then collapsed into wonderful, peaceful sleep.

An hour or two later, we were jarred awake when a band began playing in the hotel's nightclub. Even though it sounded as if the band was right outside our window, we managed to sleep fitfully, because we were so exhausted. At midnight, we heaved a sigh of relief because the band had finally quit! As it turned out, they were just taking a break. Somewhere in the wee hours of the morning they stopped and we were able to get the rest we so much craved.

The next morning we ate a plain and scant breakfast, which matched the starkness of the dining room. After a few more errands around town, we finally hit the road for Sotik— headed off to see what could possibly be our new home. Within minutes of leaving the crowded city of Nairobi, the landscape quickly changed to more of what I had envisioned Africa to look like. Skyscrapers, pavement and street signs dwindled away and were gradually replaced with picturesque huts with thatched roofs, villages and fields divided by thorny hedges. There were still people walking along the roadway, but now they were fewer in number and sometimes accompanied by cows and goats. Women carried large bundles on their heads and/or babies tied to their backs.

A couple of hours into our journey we reached the outskirts of the city of Nakuru. We pulled up to an old brick building Richard called the Cheese Factory. He explained that his wife, Cyndi, wanted him to stop there on the way home to pick up some cheese because there it was fresher, cheaper and there was more variety. We were curious about everything around us and wanted to experience as much as possible in the short time we were there, so we got out too. As soon as we did we were assaulted by a strong odor. I grew a bit disconcerted when I found out that the closer we got to the 'factory', the stronger the smell became. It was the aroma of fermenting milk (one of the necessary steps in the cheese making process). Taking a deep breath, I ventured inside and looked around politely at the various cheeses. I tried to inhale through my mouth instead of my nose; but after a while I couldn't take it anymore and motioned to Daryl that I would wait outside.

Richard finished making his purchases and we resumed our journey. We drove upward out of the Great Rift Valley; rising, twisting and turning as we went. The warm, still air from the floor of valley below turned crisp and cloudy. Even though it was late afternoon, there was what appeared to be fog on the highway. We didn't understand it because the sun was shining brightly. Then we saw a sign stating the elevation was around 7000 feet. We weren't driving through fog, but clouds. We were more than a mile above sea level.

As we traveled, there seemed to be some sort of activity ahead of us. Instead of passing the occasional person carrying bundles, there were now several people driving herds of animals before them. Alongside the road, women had spread burlap-type sacks onto the ground with brightly colored fruits and vegetables displayed on them. I had never seen produce with such vivid coloring. Richard pulled over and began to haggle over prices and laugh with the women. After a few minutes he came back with some potatoes and other produce and loaded them into the car. I asked why he chose this particular place to stop since we had passed several other produce stands like these over the past few miles. He said this town, Molo, marked the boundary where the Kipsigis people lived (the tribe we had come to observe) and he wanted to buy from 'his people'.

At this point in our journey we were about three and a half hours northwest of Nairobi. Our journey had begun on a mountainous plateau at an elevation of around 4,600 feet in the hustle and bustle of an international city. We later stopped at Nakuru, a town on the floor of the Great Rift Valley. Then we climbed up to an even higher plateau of around 6500 feet, to an area know as 'The Highlands'. Leaving Molo, we began descending the plateau on the other side. The wind abated and the air was not so chilly. As you can imagine, the scenes outside our windows shifted with each elevation change. The next view we encountered was green, lush, rolling hills carefully divided by trees and interspersed with well-worn footpaths. From a distance, the fields looked more like well-manicured lawns, but up close we could see they were actually acres upon acres of bushes. Richard told us that these 'bushes' were actually tea. It was hard to believe that the leaves from those bushes growing on these verdant, rolling hills, would eventually find their way to our homes in America through a little bag on a string.

Fields of tea being harvested / picked by hand

Now that we had turned more westward, we were beginning to see 'Sotik' on the road signs. The climate warmed at
this slightly lower elevation and the vegetation shifted and
altered, yet again. This was rich farm land where the rural folk
were able to live off of their land, generation after generation,
producing food crops, flowers, tea, cattle and children in
abundance. Richard told us what little money they made was
from selling their surplus produce, milk, eggs and cows. After
about six hours on the road, we turned off the main paved
highway, into the town of Sotik. My first impression was that it
was small and dirty.

The road we now traveled on was so eroded there was more dirt than paving material. Even at the slow speed at which we were driving, a cloud of dust kicked up, which explained the layer of dirt along the base of all the buildings. Though the town was small, many of its buildings were two-storied. They were built out of stone and plaster with glass windows. Electrical lines could be seen running to them. When I remarked to Richard that I was surprised at seeing so many two-storied buildings, he explained that the owners worked out of the bottom floor and lived on the second floor. Most of these businesses—banks, post office, police station, gas stations and shops, were flying the Kenyan flag or had a framed picture of the president on display.

There were other buildings made of wood nestled here and there amongst the stone buildings. Most of the wooden buildings did not have glass windows but merely openings with thick shutters. The buildings made of brick, stone and cement had bars over the windows and heavy gates to safely lock up the businesses at night. Most had a roof line that extended out over the sidewalk to make a deep porch. Dotted underneath these overhangs people had set up stalls to sell their wares out of the heat of the sun or inclement weather. At many of these, men were sitting at treadle sewing machines. On the wall behind them, dresses, pants and shirts were hanging on display. I was fascinated with this since I sew myself. But my sewing had always been powered by electricity, not the labor-intensive up and down motion of my own foot. I had seen pictures of sewing machines like these, but had never seen them firsthand. That experience was to occur over and over again. Things I had only heard or seen or read about in books, I was to see with my own eyes.

Richard mentioned that although the town was small, you could get most of your staples there. He then pointed out the 'butchery' shop, where they bought their fresh meat. The 'chemist' shop, where simple medicines could be purchased. As well as the dry goods stores and stalls where women sold produce and eggs. Most of the women were barefoot with a kerchief tied around their hair. A colorful printed fabric, called a *kanga*, was wrapped about their waists to protect their dresses. Many women had a baby tied onto their backs.

Nice roadside stand with a variety of produce

The babies were held in place by using another of these large, colorful, *kangas*. The child would rest face down on the woman's back with the fabric centered on the baby's bottom. One end of the cloth went up over the woman's shoulder and the other end went under her opposite arm. The two ends met together at the chest, where they were tied together in a large knot. This formed a snug sling which held the child close out of harm's way. This also freed up the woman's hands to sell her merchandise or to tend to whatever task she needed to. I thought that was ingenious! Another thing the ladies did to free up their hands was to carry things balanced on their heads (in much the same manner that young ladies balance books on their heads to promote good posture). Both of these things seemed so out of the ordinary to me that I couldn't imagine walking up to one of these ladies and actually buying something from their hand. Yet, I knew that if we chose to live here, I would need to learn how. After all, food is difficult to live without.

We turned off the main street through town, which was becoming less and less paved, onto a road which was now completely dirt. That road took us by a third gas station. It was hard to believe a town that small could support one gas station, let alone three. Richard assured us that even though the city itself was small it serviced a large area and sold more than just gasoline, or petrol as it was called. The stations also sold kerosene, which was what the majority of people used to power their lanterns, diesel for the delivery trucks and propane cylinders of cooking fuel. We left that dirt road for a narrower, rutted one and passed quickly out of the town. A short time later, we came to a stop beside a vine covered stone cottage.

"We're home!" Richard happily announced.

We started pulling out bags and parcels and headed inside to meet the rest of the family. Before we even made it to the door, Cyndi, Richard's wife, came out to warmly welcome us, followed soon afterwards by their children, Heather, Aaron and Naomi. Working together, we quickly got the truck unloaded. They then gave us a quick tour of their home. It was small and I wondered where we would sleep. The only space that seemed available was on the living room floor. About that time, Cyndi let us know that we'd be staying at the 'Van Rheenen house' while we were there.

The Van Rheenens were the first family from the 'Old

Sotik Team' to leave for America. Since houses that had both electricity and running water were hard to come by in that area, they had decided to keep renting the house until our team arrived. One of our four families from the 'New Sotik Team' would eventually live in that house, but we didn't know which one as of yet. While we were unloading the truck, I had caught glimpses of a roofline through the hedges that served as a boundary between the two properties. I realized that must be the 'Van Rheenen house' she spoke of. I was grateful to know we would have a bed instead of the floor, but I was still a bit uneasy about staying by ourselves, deep in the heart of Africa!

Cyndi told us we'd be eating supper with them that night and then with the Allison family the following night. In fact, they had made tentative arrangements for our evening meal for almost every day of our stay. She went on to explain that for our breakfasts and lunches, we would be on our own. I wasn't prepared for this and felt a little blindsided. Cyndi must have noticed my 'deer caught in a head light look' because she quickly told me not to worry because she had stocked the pantry and refrigerator with some things.

Passing between the hedges, we were shown our 'home' for the next few weeks. The kitchen appliances were smaller and a little different than what we were used to, so Cyndi showed us how they all worked. Then she pointed out the pantry where there was a small box of cereal, a small brown paper bag of sugar, tea bags, small bananas the size of your finger, oranges, red onions, potatoes, avocados and tomatoes. In the refrigerator there was water, milk, butter, cheese, bread, jam, brown eggs, carrots, lettuce and some sandwich meat. I felt a flood of relief as I realized I wouldn't need to deal with buying any food just yet, since she had so thoroughly anticipated our needs and had supplied us so well.

Cyndi then took us outside to show us how the hot water heater worked. It struck me as odd that we were going outside to do this until I saw that the water tank was built into the outer wall of the house. There was a stack of firewood beside it and a fireplace type opening underneath it. Cyndi warned us that it was better to heat the water slowly. If the water heated too quickly, it would be orange from the rust inside the water tank.

"You need to plan ahead when you want to take a hot bath or shower because it takes about twenty to thirty minutes for the water to heat up properly," she explained.

As I stood there thinking, *"I've never built a fire in my life,"* she said she was off to put the finishing touches on supper. After she left, Daryl patted me on the shoulder, knowing my concern and said, "Don't worry, I'll build the fires."

We brought our suitcases into the bedroom and put our things away in the built-in dresser inside the closet and then looked around the rest of the house. It was bigger than the Chowning's house and was simply furnished with just the basics we would need. Now, instead of feeling somewhat abandoned, I realized they were only trying to give us some privacy. By having us stay on our own, it allowed us the space we needed to process what we would be experiencing, without people around us 24/7. We were grateful for that.

Over the evening meal, they told us that Fielden Allison, the other member of their team, would be coming the next morning for the men's regularly scheduled business meeting. Richard added that they wanted to use part of their time to go over the plans they'd made for us. After dinner, we visited for a bit longer. About an hour later, we went back to 'our house' with the aid of a flashlight and settled in for the night.

The next morning, Fielden and another man, Mark Berry-man, a single missionary, joined us. Mark had taken groups of people all over Africa on survey trips and was currently assisting the Sotik Team in between projects. The four men and I sat down together at the Chowning's dining table to go over the itinerary they set for us. There were a few open dates because they didn't want to overwhelm us. During the discussion, Cyndi served us tea with something to eat and also gave her input on a few items on our itinerary. We agreed to all they had planned. We even filled in some of the blank spaces with activities Mark suggested that we do. All of these plans were exciting to us because we were beginning to see our thoughts and dreams become reality.

Simple wooden shops or 'dukas'

   Out of everything on the itinerary, we were especially looking forward to two things. One activity was an overnight stay in a nearby Kipsigis village for three days and three nights, for what we called a 'mini-bond.' A mini-bond is a short period of time in which you are to immerse yourself in the local culture, to 'bond' with it. You use this time to try to absorb as much of the culture and language as you can without the distractions or 'crutch' of your own culture. The second activity we were looking forward to was a possible day trip to the famous Maasai Mara Game Reserve.

With these plans in place, they gave us the rest of the afternoon off to further acclimate ourselves. They suggested we walk into the town of Sotik, just to have a look around 'up-close and personal.' We confirmed the time of the evening meal that night with Fielden and his family. Mark was to pick us up since he was also joining them for dinner. We told everyone goodbye and headed back to our house to grab a bite to eat before setting off to explore.

Entering our home through the kitchen door, we looked at the food around us unenthusiastically because neither of us was very hungry. Besides the fact that Cyndi had recently fed us a large snack during our meeting with the guys at tea time, our appetites were off because our 'body clocks' were not on schedule. I was too excited to eat anyway and wanted to start exploring Sotik. Daryl was still drained from jet lag and wanted nothing more than to take a nap before he could even think about exploring. Even though the clock said 1 p.m. local time, our bodies thought it was 8 p.m. Daryl set the alarm, fearing he may sleep the afternoon away and then wouldn't be able to sleep that night. Like usual, he conked out right away.

Since I wasn't adventurous enough to explore by myself, I decided to busy myself with other activities—writing things down in the notebook, going over the itinerary again, washing out clothes, etc. Those tasks were quickly done, so I checked on Daryl and found him still sleeping. Cyndi had thoughtfully left books on a shelf for our reading pleasure. Most of them seemed to be about people who had lived in Kenya. The one I chose was called, *Shadows on the Grass*, written by Isak Dinesen.

This is the pen name for Baroness Karen von Blixen-Finecke whose book, *Out of Africa,* had recently become very popular.

Stretching out beside Daryl, I relaxed and leisurely read, wondering if Kenya would some day make as strong an impression on me as it had on her. Before I realized it, I drifted off to sleep, too. When the alarm went off, it was a real struggle for us to wake up. We splashed water on our faces, made a quick sandwich and grabbed some fruit as we headed out the door. With notebook in hand, Kenya shillings in our pockets and butterflies in my stomach, we set off to walk into Sotik to check out the place that we might one day call 'home.'

Back view of a five shilling note, Tano is five in Kiswahili

LESSON LEARNED

Sometimes it is unsettling when your dreams are becoming reality. But, if you let those uncertain feelings hold you back, all you'll have are your wishes and worries. Not the true experiences you were meant to have.

THREE

somok

(so moke)

*"This is it! If I take one more step, it will be
the farthest away from home I've ever been."*
Movie: Lord of the Rings

MOMENTS OF CLARITY

Africa is a place unlike any other; one moment it seems awkward and behind; in another advanced and refined. There are
so many things to discover about it and yourself while you are
there. A few of the things we experienced stand out with crystal
clear clarity. Like the first time I approached a 'real live' mud
hut. As I did so, I seemed to have this commentary running
through my head. *"I'm walking up to a real, African hut...I'm
going inside a real, African hut...I am sitting inside a real,
African hut...I'm not just seeing this on the TV; I'm really doing
this...ME!"* It had an almost surreal quality to it because it felt
more like I was walking onto a movie set instead of entering an
actual home. I remember wanting to reach up and touch the
grass of the roof as I ducked into the doorway to enter the hut.

I wasn't sure if they would be offended if I did, so I decided not to at that time.

Once inside, I couldn't resist the temptation to touch the walls. I casually rested my hand on the wall behind my back, feeling its coolness and solidity. As I looked about the inside of the hut, its simplicity and cleanliness surprised me. The dirt floor was hard and compacted over years of use, but as clean and tidy as a cement floor. The benches and chairs we sat on were handcrafted, not mass produced in a factory. There was a painted table, well-worn but scrubbed clean, in the middle of the hut. In America, we would call these furnishings, 'shabby chic' and pay quite a bit of money to achieve the same effect.

With quiet dignity and shy grace, we were warmly greeted and received by the occupants of the home and the people who lived nearby. Not only that place, but everywhere we went. Since there were no TVs or other distractions, our arrivals became the big event of the village. Kids flocked from all over to stare at the visitors. Adults were more restrained in their curiosity. They simply looked up from their work in the fields as we passed by, waving or calling out a greeting to let us know we were welcomed.

One evening we were visiting with a group of people and as usual were packed tightly together in a hut. There was no electricity so a kerosene lantern had been lit and was hanging from a hook in the rafters. As conversations ebbed and flowed around us, we managed to pick up a word here and there. Mark, our guide for the evening, translated for us whenever he could.

After a while, Mark turned to us and said, "They have requested that we sing them a song in English. I thought that maybe the two of you could sing a duet. Do you know how to sing in two-part harmony? They don't really sing that way here and I think they would enjoy hearing it. Could you do that?"

After answering, "Yes," we asked for a minute to figure out what to sing.

Even though you carry around hundreds of tunes in your head, when asked to sing from memory, it's hard to think of a single one. Daryl and I both grew up in churches where a Sunday Singing Night—a worship service spent in songs of praise—were regularly held. Daryl, who has a beautiful tenor voice, had many occasions to lead songs, so he was comfortable in this setting. I grew up in a singing family. We often had others over for 'a singing' and would try to learn new songs. So, I too didn't mind singing in front of others either.

We quietly started and stopped several songs between the two of us, trying to remember the words and to figure out what to sing. After a bit, we decided on the song, <u>Can You Count</u>

the Stars? We chose this song because it had a simple tune that the two of us could carry. But more importantly, we could remember all of its words.

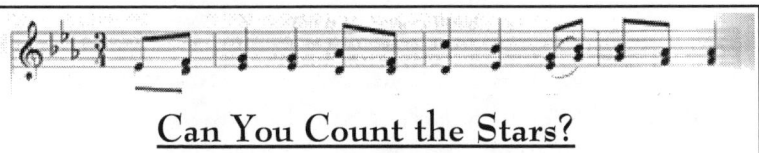

Can You Count the Stars?

Can you count the stars of evening that are shining in the sky?
Can you count the clouds that daily over all the world goes by?

> God the Lord, who doth not slumber,
> Keepeth all the boundless number:
> But He careth more for thee
> But He careth more for thee

Can you count the birds that warble in the sunshine all the day?
Can you count the little fishes that in sparkling waters play?

> God the Lord their number knoweth,
> For each one His care He showeth:
> Shall He not remember thee?
> Shall He not remember thee?

Can you count the many children in their little beds at night?
Who without a thought of sorrow rise again at morning light?

> God the Lord who dwells in heaven,
> Loving care to each has given,
> He has not forgotten thee.
> He has not forgotten thee.

German Folk Tune   **Johann Hey**

I'll never forget the utter stillness, the rapt attention of the villagers, young and old alike as we sang. That last note seemed to hang about, suspended in the air, when we finished.

We sat there—us looking at them, them looking back at us—burning this evening and this moment into our memories. When they realized we were finished, they clapped with big grins on their faces, avidly nodding their heads. I don't know how many of them even understood English, but they acted as though we had just given them a fine gift. The sweetness of the moment drew us to them as a people we would like to live among.

The time finally came for our 'mini-bond'. The Kenyan family we were to stay with lived in the village of Chemabei. The missionaries drove us to a house to share in a meal, like they had many times before. But this time, they drove away, leaving us behind to interact, communicate and sleep on our own with no way to contact them until they returned to get us. We were staying at the home of David and Mary Sambu.

The area where they lived was rural but a more affluent region of the Kipsigis tribe. That was because they were able to grow tea as a cash crop, which was more lucrative than produce. The extra money allowed them to send their kids to boarding school to receive a better education. Yet, the Sambus and most of their neighbors still lived in mud huts. Even though it was made of mud, there were signs of affluence all around them. They had a cooking hut that was separate from the living/sleeping house. There was corrugated tin rather than grass on their roof. The patch of land that surrounded their house had grass growing on it instead of vegetables. And more importantly to us at the time, the entire Sambu family spoke English.

That evening after supper we visited with the family and then headed to bed early. We were pleasantly surprised when we were shown to a bedroom off of the main room of the living/sleeping hut. That room had a small wooden bed for us to share. We had planned to sleep on the floor in the main room (like we thought would happen at the Chowning's) and had brought sleeping bags for that very purpose. But again, we were given privacy when we were not expecting it. The next morning we shared a simple breakfast of bread and butter sandwiches and *chaik* with lots of milk and sugar. After breakfast, Daryl accompanied David into the village, while Mary took me by the hand into her cooking hut. Someone had obviously made Mary and her family aware that we were trying to learn as much as possible about the Kipsigis culture. Because as Mary would do some chore, she explained what, how and why she was doing it. Then she would hand it over to me and tell me to give it a try. There was a lot of laughter at my expense when she realized I didn't have a clue as to how to do many of the things she did on a daily basis: things like chopping wood, starting a fire and then cooking over the fire pit.

cooking kimiyet--corn meal, over a wood fire

Mary continued to add twigs and to chop larger chunks of wood with a *panga*—machete. She gently blew on the embers to keep the fire burning at the desired heat. Then she put in the proper amounts of ingredients into large metal cooking pots to make *chaik* or *kimiyet*. *Kimiyet* is a cornmeal and water mixture (similar to grits) that is cooked by stirring it constantly with a large wooden spoon (like a small, short oar), until all the water is absorbed. Once this is done, the mixture is now firm and can be inverted onto a plate and cut with a knife. *Kimiyet* is the Kenyan's daily 'bread' and can be served along with *chaik* any time of the day or night.

When I was handed a homemade broom made of branches to sweep out the cooking hut, I thought, "*Finally, something I know how to do!*" So I began brushing the dirt floors with gusto only to hear Mary say, "No, no! Too much dust." She then showed me how I should first sprinkle the floor with water and then *gently* brush the dirt floor.

But what caused the most laughter (from me as well) was when she sent me to the river with her daughters to get water. Each girl carried an empty five-gallon container called a 'jerry can'. The original jerry cans were olive drab metal containers which were strapped onto vehicles to carry extra water when traveling out in 'the bush'. You definitely wouldn't want to be stuck out in the middle of nowhere with an over-heated engine and a mud puddle as your only source of water to fill it. The modern day counterpart to this still bears some resemblance in its basic shape and form. But they are now made of plastic and come in a rainbow assortment of colors. The ones we took to the river that day were sky blue, faded pink and bright yellow.

We traveled a wooded, well-worn path until we came to a quiet, trickling stream. The girls showed me how to lay the jerry can on its side in the stream and push it down until the trapped air inside bubbled out and then began to fill with water. While we waited for the containers to fill up, they started looking around the ground for large leaves. (On an earlier visit to another village, I had closely watched the women do this same thing.) The leaves they gathered were overlapped then tightly rolled into a circle like an oversized donut. This 'leaf donut' served as a cushion and leveler between the flat bottom of the jerry can and the round shape of the human head. These girls didn't know I knew about this little cushion, so you can imagine their surprise when I started to twist the leaves into the appropriate shape. They giggled shyly, nodding their heads with satisfaction. After each container became full, it was pulled out of the stream and the next container put in its place. As we waited for the next one to fill, they would top off the previous one with a small milk pail and then the cap was securely screwed on. The now full container was set to the side. Lastly, the pail used for topping off the containers was also filled.

Next came the arduous job of lifting those five-gallon containers of water up over head and shoulders to come to gently rest on the top of their heads. I watched this graceful display until they turned to me and handed me the little milking pail. I held it by the handle and immediately felt the pulling weight of the water on my arm. As I turned towards the path, they stopped me, pointed to my head and then handed me a leaf donut. They took the pail from my hand and helped me to balance it on my head. I was amazed by two things: first, how light the pail felt on top of my head compared to the pulling weight on my arm; and secondly, that this entire interchange had been carried out as they maintained the balance of their containers of water on their heads.

As we started back home, I ran into a problem. Every time I looked down to keep from stubbing my toe or tripping over roots in my path, water spilled out of the bucket and down the front of my shirt. I tried to glance down without moving my head, but even this slight movement caused the water to spill. I gave up trying to balance the bucket and just held it in place by hand. As I slowly walked to the hut with the girls, I wondered what kinds of things the men were doing and thought, "*I wish Daryl could see me doing this!*" One of the girls must have told Mary about me spilling water because she was waiting outside for me with a big grin on her face as I approached the hut. She helped me remove the pail from my head and dumped the water into a 55-gallon drum used for water storage.

She held up the little pail and chuckled, "This is what the little girls use when they are first learning to carry water." I asked her what age that was. When she said around five or six years old, it made me feel gawky and clumsy!

Mary asked, "Haven't you ever carried water before?"

"No." I replied.

"Do you collect rainwater?" She asked.

Again, my answer was, "No."

"Do you get your water from a well?" Mary persisted.

I simply shook my head, no.

"Then where does your water come from?" Mary asked, wondering how we got out water.

When I explained that I just turned on the faucet and the water came out, she looked confused. So, I pantomimed the action to try to clarify. Finally, she grinned and said, "Oh, the *tap*. Yes, we have water at the school like that, but not at someone's home!" Having solved that matter, Mary stopped peppering me with questions.

Now it was my turn. I asked her, "How do you carry the water bucket and not get water all over you?"

Mary explained that most of the containers have lids that screwed on so normally it was not a problem. I nodded, but again I asked about the pail. At this, Mary put some water in the pail from the drum and told me to carry it. She watched me as I self-consciously walked in front of her.

"Don't look down," she instructed me.

"But, how can I see where I'm going?" I asked.

"Don't look down at your feet while you are walking. Look out at the path to see what is ahead of you." She said, which sounded like a good lesson to use for life.

Kenyan stamp depicting women carrying water

She pretended to carry a bucket and demonstrated the proper technique and position to hold your head. I copied her, much to the delight of the giggling spectators, until I received Mary's nod of approval. Now satisfied, she sent me inside to change out of my wet things. When I went in the hut I expected to see Daryl but he wasn't there. If he had been, I'm sure all the giggling would have drawn him outside.

Once again in dry clothes, I came out of the hut and draped my wet shirt on a nearby bush to dry, as was the practice. Turning towards Mary, I saw her pointing out other houses in the village to a man. As they conversed, a girl brought him a cup of water in an enamel mug. (To cut down on water-borne diseases, drinking water was boiled then placed in a covered crock inside the hut. While we had been at the stream getting water, a cow had ambled up and stopped in the middle of it to get a drink before crossing over to the other side. As it stood there drinking, it also urinated. Thankfully, it was 'down river' so the urine flowed away from us.)

Since I had so recently helped in making the fire in the cooking hut and carrying water from the stream, I realized what a labor-intensive effort this simple cup of water was. First, you had to haul the water from the river, boil it over a wood fire with scrap wood you had to gather and carry to your house, and then finally you stored the water in a special container in the house. Instead of a chipped mug of water, I felt as if she was presenting him with a golden goblet of nectar!

It was a little warm standing out in the sun, so we moved to sit under the shade of the nearby trees. Permanent benches had been built there by nailing long planks of wood onto low short posts buried in the ground. David Sambu was a head-master of a local school and a leader in the church; thereby making him a respected leader in the community. This man may have been there to seek David's advice since he was so highly respected. These backless 'benches' were used for David to meet with people and were built to accommodate the crowds from the church and community that sometimes gathered at their home. After a lull in the conversation, he took another sip of water and then tossed the remainder onto the ground.

I wanted to jump off the bench and say, *"What do you think you are doing? Don't you realize there's no plumbing in this house? They have to go down to the river and haul back every drop! How could you throw it so casually to the ground as if it was nothing?"* But I didn't. We were told the Kipsigis people did not under _any_ circumstances show anger, or any other great display of emotion, for that matter. So instead, I kept my thoughts to myself, looking at the faces around me.

Everyone seemed completely at ease, with no sign of displeasure whatsoever. *"Of, course!"* I realized. *"This _is_ just water to them. How else would water get to the hut except for a woman to haul it up from the river? Why should he or these ladies see their effort as anything special? After all, it is just a common daily occurrence to them. It is me, seeing from my privileged western view that thinks of this as something extra-ordinary.*" While I was processing all of this, the man rose to shake everyone's hand before going.

I managed to pull myself together and say the proper parting word, '*Saisere*—goodbye."

Mary picked up the cup to take inside the hut for washing later and I followed her. Once inside the cooking hut, we began chopping vegetables for the evening meal. As we worked and discussed different things, I rather hesitantly asked, "Mary, how do you feel when someone doesn't finish their water and throws it on the ground after it's been carried up from the river?"

Without even pausing in her task, her simple response was, "That's women's work."

It wasn't said with malice or contempt, the way I probably would have said it. She spoke the statement in the manner of '*that's the way it is, that's the way it's always been and that's the way it will continue to be*'. This affirmed my earlier thought that this was just an everyday occurrence to them. Living in a developing nation opens your eyes to many things that we often take for granted. An acquaintance of mine had a sign hanging above her kitchen sink which read: *Live simply so others can simply live.* She had it hanging there so she could think about it while she washed her dishes by hand instead of using an automatic dishwasher.

Lesson Learned

Try not to take the simple things, like water, for granted. For lots of people, it's a daily struggle just to obtain it.

[Another job considered 'women's work]

First, men frame the house & then women 'mal' it. To 'mal', you make and stack big mud balls in between the wooden timber frames until it forms a wall.

After the mud dries, the hut is smeared inside and out with a thin watered down mud mixture of different colors to create a decorative pattern.

Kathy Rogers and I are helping our (the Bates') language teacher, Antony, with his new house.

FOUR

ang'wan

(ahng wan)

"Why are you being so polite?"

"For the same reason you are not.
It was the way I was raised."
Movie: Twelve Angry Men

THE VILLAGE
ELDERS DECIDE

Our husbands returned as dusk was falling. After greeting the men, Mary shooed me out of the cooking hut, telling me to visit with the men. Entering the living/sleeping hut, I found that David had lit a kerosene lamp and was in the process of hanging it from a hook in the ceiling. Without the lamp it would have been pitch black since they and everyone else around them did not have electricity. You tend to forget how much difference a single light can make when it is so dark. After hanging the lamp, David went back into his bedroom. In a bit, he came back out with a battery operated radio so we could listen to the evening news. What a treat! Other than listening to the car radio, I could not remember the last time I had just sat and listened to the news via radio.

The telecast alternated between English and Kiswahili. Whenever something was said in Kiswahili, but not in English, David translated for us. When the telecast was over, David left it on so we could listen to the local music now playing on the station. Just at that time, Mary brought in supper and we all ate together in the large multi-purpose room. As we ate, David told Mary some of the news he'd heard on the radio. When we were done, I stood up to help Mary with the dishes, but she said, "No. Stay. You are the visitor."

David again slipped into his room, returning this time with pictures. Mary came back shortly after giving the cleanup duty to one of her daughters and joined in the discussion as David showed us their pictures. Mary told the guys about our day after we were finished looking at the pictures. Everyone had a good laugh over my water carrying ability. David said they didn't have anything like that to report. They had just gone about the village deciding how we would spend the remaining time we had with them. After a while, we all decided to go to bed. David took the lamp with him to his room after Daryl and I reached the door of our room. Getting ready for bed with the aid of a flashlight, we squeezed ourselves onto the narrow cot. Cramped, but thankful we were not on the floor, we quietly chatted about the day until we drifted off to sleep.

It seemed that the plan they worked out for the next day, was for us to visit every house in the village! Everywhere we stopped there was something to eat, drink, or both. We passed the time in much the same manner at each hut. We sang songs together in the Kipsigis language (as best as we could). Children, who were taught English in school, would shyly sing to us, accompanied with a lot of nervous laughing and hiding of their faces behind hands, the crook of their arm or each other.

We prayed together, talked about the Bible or just sat around visiting with each other. They asked us questions about America and we asked about Kenya. It was funny when they said Kenyans thought everyone in America walked around with guns strapped to their hips. They thought it was humorous when we told them, people in America thought Africans walked around wearing animal skins. We were amused by the misconceptions we both had about each other's countries.

Making our way to yet another hut in the village, an old woman waved for us to come her way. The Kenyan man traveling around with us as our interpreter and guide seemed taken aback. As we drew nearer, we saw her yard and hut more clearly. They didn't seem to be in very good condition, like the other houses we had seen. Even the wooden spike, which normally stood proudly out of the top of the thatched roofs of their huts, was broken and askew. (We found out later that this signified that the man of the house had died.) As they talked together, we caught the words *wazungu*—white people, and *toek*—visitors. After another moment, she turned and went back into her hut. We figured she was just curious about who we were and had flagged us down just to get a closer look.

We expected the guide to motion for us continue on our way. But he just stood there with a slightly perplexed look on his face. I wondered if she had said something insulting about us and he was just too polite to say anything. Much to my surprise, he instructed us to have a seat on the grass, stating that we were to be honored with a special treat. I sat and worried that this poor woman would go hungry because she was serving us something she needed to save for herself.

After a short wait, she came out resplendent in leather hides and long beaded earrings. The ear decorations were leather strips about one inch wide and six inches long. They were draped over the lower portion of her stretched out earlobes which caused the beaded strips to come to rest on her shoulders.

The garment had been elaborately embellished with beads, shells, porcupine quills and other adornment. It looked similar in design to items worn by Native Americans. But instead of soft supple leather, her garment was stiff. It also still had the hair on it looked which made it look more like an animal hide.

Our host explained that this was the ceremonial 'coming out' garment that she had worn when she was as a teenage girl at her initiation ceremony. That ceremony was the way to announce to one and all that she was now a woman and eligible for marriage. He told us we were very privileged to have seen this. It was very rare for these garments to be brought out for show. We *were* suitably impressed and asked permission to take her photo. She agreed and arranged her garments just so. Sitting as regal as a queen on the grass with her hut falling to ruins behind her, we took her picture.

Afterwards, she shook our hands from where she sat, while we said, "*Kongoi, kongoi mising*—thank you, thank you very much!" She nodded her head again in a majestic manner, remaining seated as our guide motioned for us to leave. We assumed that since she didn't have food to share, she shared her most prized possession with us instead.

By late afternoon, we were surprised to see Fielden Allison enter the hut we were then in. He warmly greeted our group and jokingly explained how he had to go to every hut in the village to find us. As was the custom, he was offered something to eat. Fielden grabbed his stomach and faked a groan, saying, "Oh! Didn't I just say I had been to every hut?!"

Everyone laughed. But because it was a great faux pas to not eat what was served you, Fielden took a small portion. This served as a 'sign' that he accepted their hospitality and made everyone happy. After chatting with one and all for a bit, Fielden said he wanted to speak with us. Stepping outside, he asked us how things were going and we told him we were really enjoying ourselves.

He responded, "Good. We knew this would be a good place for you to stay because everyone is so hospitable and so many in this area know English."

Red dirt road meandering through lush green hills

Fielden went on to explain that something had come up and he wanted to see how we felt about it. Things had worked out so that we had an opportunity to go with him and his family to the Maasai Mara Game Park after all. But, we would need to leave that day, cutting our time in the village short. Fielden had come by to find out if we still wanted to go to the game park or if we would rather stay in the village.

"The game park!" we both chimed.

He said that he thought we would say that, but first he needed to speak with David before we could leave. We all went back inside the hut we had just left. Fielden gave his goodbyes to everyone there and then left. We stayed inside and continued with our visit. He was gone for quite some time. We didn't think much about it since the Kipsigis loved to sit and talk!

When he did eventually returned, Fielden spoke in Kipsigis to our hosts and then motioned for us to leave with him. We told everyone goodbye and left.

On our way to the Sambu's, I told him, "It won't take us long to throw our stuff together. When do you want to go?"

Surprisingly, he replied, "You may not be able to go."

"Why?" we asked.

Fielden answered. "The village elders decide if and when you will leave."

"Why? Are they going with us?" I asked.

"No," he said.

"Then what difference does it make to them if we go or if we stay?" I continued, not understanding.

He explained that as long as we were guests of the village, we were under the care and watch of the entire village. The decision for us to come and stay with the Sambu Family had been the village's decision. Therefore, it would be a village decision for us to leave as well. This type of group decision making process involving the whole village seemed so foreign to me. Then it hit me. It seemed foreign because it was foreign! When we go to an unfamiliar country, we expect things to look, sound, smell, taste and even feel differently. But, for some strange reason, we don't expect the people to *think* any differently than we do! Then when they do think in another way, we don't understand what's going on.

We arrived at the Sambu's house and waited for David to get back from the meeting with the elders. While we waited, I tried to prepare myself for the possibility that we may not get to go. That got me to thinking. *"How will I react if they say no? Will I argue and complain? Would it make any difference if I did? Will I be gracious only if the answer is the one I want to hear?"* Finally, to put an end to my musings, I told myself, *"We're staying in the village. That's why we've come isn't it?"*

Arriving soon after that, David called us to him to explain the decision of the tribal elders. "Since there is a meeting already scheduled for this evening, everyone will expect you to be there. Many of the people will have walked a long distance to come. We can't disappoint them. Also, everyone knows how long you were to stay with us in our care. How will it look if you leave before the time is up? They will think something amiss happened to make you leave early. On the other hand, they understand that you would like to see as much of our country in the short time you have here. So, after the meeting tonight, we will announce to everyone why you are leaving. Then everyone will understand and you will be free to go!"

There were smiles all around when he finished explaining. I could see why David was such a respected leader. He made sure that each one gave and took a little so that everyone was happy. I must admit, I gave a huge sigh of relief when he said we would be allowed to leave that night! Quickly, we pulled our things together and said our goodbyes before going to the meeting. But before we left, Mary insisted we stay for one more cup of tea!

The meeting ran late into the night. Because of the belated hour, Fielden brought us to his house to sleep. That saved time both tonight and in the morning. The Allison family lived in the city of Litein, which is about fifteen to twenty minutes from the city of Sotik where we were staying. It was nearly midnight by the time we finally got settled in and lay down to rest. We left at dawn the next morning, so our rest was a short one. The game park trip was a quick one-day safari. We traveled to the park, drove all over it and then returned that same day. On American roads, that may seem simple enough, but what an arduous undertaking it was!! The Allison's vehicle had a cushioned bench seat up front and an enclosed long truck bed on the back. There were no cushioned seats in the back of the truck, but long wooden benches running its length and facing each other. For short excursions on dirt roads or even a long trip into Nairobi on bumpy paved roads, the ride wasn't too bad. But off-roading on washboard dirt tracks was a bone-jarring sensation I had never experienced the likes of before! All discomfort was forgotten however, with that first glimpse of animals in the wild.

As with many things in Africa, the reversal of what you would expect was what actually happened. In the Game Park, *we* were the ones that stayed in the enclosed area while the animals were free to roam, or stop and look curiously at us. Because there are no fences or visible boundaries, we actually saw wild animals before we got to the park. When you are inside the designated boundaries of the game park, you are to keep to the paths carved out of the bush by the park and not veer off of them. But outside of the park, the rules of the park do not yet apply.

Coming upon a giraffe beside the road on our way to the park, Fielden slowed down and crept up to it. When we got too close for its comfort, it ran off. Baby giraffe are six feet tall when they are born. Adult giraffe average twelve feet tall. I had no idea how big that one was but it was enormous. With its legs taking up most of this measurement, they were the same height as the truck!

Looking out the front windshield of the truck as we gave chase, all you could see were long, spotted, loping legs. What a sight! Another lone animal we came across outside the park was an elephant. Again Fielden tried to get as close as possible. This elephant however, didn't turn and run like the giraffe had. Instead, he turned toward us and stood his ground. As we slowly crept, ever closer, he started flapping his ears and stirring up dust; a sure sign he was getting agitated. Fielden's kids, who were with us in the back of the truck and getting nervous, asked him to stop. Fielden gave a chuckle and backed off just as the elephant raised his trunk. They told us that is what elephants do as a warning before they charge.

Once we went through the gate of the park, it wasn't long before we began seeing animals in herds instead of singly. There is nothing quite like seeing something up close and 'in the flesh' as opposed to reading about it or seeing it on TV. When you see animals out of their natural habitat, you wonder how on earth their markings can serve as protection. Their markings seem to draw attention instead of acting as camouflage. But in their natural environment, they blend in with their surroundings and they can hide in plain sight.

We broke up our long day by stopping at one of the many game lodges that are scattered throughout the park. These lodges are where visitors to the park can stay to sleep for the night or several nights. They range from simple tents to expensive suites with all the modern conveniences. Most have a wonderful buffet luncheon complete with sodas over ice. The one where we stopped is called *Kechwa Tembo*—The Elephant's Skull. The lodge had an elephant's skull, minus its tusks, placed at the entrance as you drove in. Sitting at our table, we enjoyed the expansive view of the plains, the great food and the break from the bumpy truck. Someone from our party flagged down the waiter to ask him for more ice.

He said, "Yes, you Americans like lots of ice." We all thought that was funny. Whenever he would pass by our table he'd jokingly ask, "More ice?" We would just smile and shake our heads no.

We were amazed at how nice everything was. Janet explained that it was like that for the tourist business, which is Kenya's number one source of income. She further explained to us that everything was either trucked in on huge trucks or was flown in because the animals ate up the gardens. Once we received the bill, we understood a little better how they could afford to charge the prices they did. But it was still worth it. There's nothing like an ice cold soda when you've been bouncing around in the back of a dusty truck for hours on end.

That game park safari was without a doubt one of the high points of our survey trip. There were many other things we enjoyed and saw during the few weeks we were there. We got to spend time in the village with Kenyans. We lived on our own, cooking our own meals, shopping for food and washing our clothes by hand. We even borrowed a vehicle and drove into the nearby town of Kericho by ourselves, to go to the movies. We really felt like we got an understanding of what it would be like to live there and we were truly grateful for that.

Even when my experiences were not good, I was thankful for those, too. Towards the end of our stay, we walked by ourselves to the nearby village of Chebongi. As we stood in the doorway of someone's hut, the city of Sotik was pointed out to us. Seeing how close we were to 'home', I suddenly had an overwhelming desire to just get out of there. I found a moment to whisper privately to Daryl, "I feel kind of funny. I think I'm going to go back to the house."

I'm sure he was shocked when I said that. I am notorious for my awful sense of direction. Because I do get lost easily, I don't like to travel by myself. When I do travel alone, I like to have a map or explicit directions to keep me on track.

He said, "I really don't think we should leave right now." But there must have been some kind of expression on my face, because he added, "If I stay, do you really think you can find your way back by yourself?"

When I smiled with relief and told him it didn't look too difficult, he didn't try to change my mind. He just reviewed the paths we have just taken, to make sure I would be able to make my way back and told me what to say in Kipsigis to our hosts.

I made my excuses by saying, "*Makaran moet. Amache awendi ga*—My stomach isn't good. I need to go home."

View from a hut in Chebongi, white dots on the hill is the sun reflecting off of tin roofs from houses near Sotik

Starting out, I was nervous and unsure of myself. Nevertheless as I saw things along the way that I remembered, I grew more confident. The closer I got to town; strangely, the better I felt. Once I got to town, it was easy to find my way to the house because Sotik is so small. Finally getting home, I lay down, but soon realized I didn't feel unwell after all. So I got up and started working on dinner. When Daryl returned, a couple of hours later, I told him about my experience. His response was that I was probably feeling some 'culture shock'.

I told him, "I don't know what it was. But, I just felt that if I had to drink one more cup of *chaik* or sing one more, loud, monotone Kipsigis song, I thought I would scream!"

He said, "Yeah, I'd say that was culture shock!"

Soon after that we were able to attend a missionary meeting. It was good to see how missionaries in other parts of the country lived. Once a month or at least bi-monthly, the missionaries got together for a meeting. These gave opportunities to visit with other Americans/missionaries, to get a break from your own area and to talk over the things that were working and things that weren't. That month, the meeting was being held in Eldoret. Being one of the larger cities in the country, it had lots of modern stores. Eldoret offered a greater variety of products, appliances, furniture and clothing. It even had a golf club where there was a swimming pool, tennis courts and a place to get a bite to eat. The city was so large it had a maze of paved streets. I couldn't believe the differences between the two towns! It was like a miniature Nairobi.

When I went into the Eldoret missionaries' houses, those were different too. Their houses were primarily furnished with American things with a few African accents here and there. Many had American appliances. When I questioned the Eldoret ladies about their choice of furnishings, they said that after being out in the 'bush' all day; they wanted to create an American-type oasis to come home to. So they had furnished their houses with as many American furnishings as they could.

As strange as this may sound, that really touched me. I thought, "*Now this is something that I can do!*" With my background in Interior Decorating I felt inept at the thought of becoming a missionary. I wondered what 'talents' I could bring to the team. Now, I was excited to finally find something that I was able to do that could potentially help our team. With tablet in hand, I talked to as many people as I could, asking them questions like: "What is something you're thankful you brought over from the States? What is something you wish you had brought over but forgot to? Why did you choose those items?"

Anything I thought to ask I did. I was like a dog with a bone, but after a while, I got a headache and had to stop. Even in that I was grateful. I get migraines and usually have to take medicine and lie down before it will go away. I had forgotten to bring anything with me on that trip, but the missionary wives took care of me. They gave me some medicine purchased locally called Hedex®, which is similar to migraine medicine in the States and then found me a quiet place to rest. After an hour or so, I felt much better and was able to rejoin the others.

The reason I was thankful was that even with migraines, I still found a way to function and it wouldn't hold me back from moving to Kenya. Everything that occurred on our survey trip reinforced in me the desire to come and work among these gentle, reserved and gracious people. Meeting with other missionaries, also reinforced in me that it takes all kinds of people to come to the mission field. God only asks for an open and willing heart so that _He_ can be seen working in you. I found this much quoted phrase to be true, 'God doesn't call the equipped, He equips the called.'

LESSON LEARNED

*Sometimes the best gift you can give is the gift of yourself.
Whether you are the recipient of the gift or the giver,
receive it or give it with the honor and respect it deserves.*

FIVE

mut

(moot)

*"If you need something, get it yourself,
or better yet, learn to live without."*
Movie: <u>Secondhand Lions</u>

READY OR NOT

When we returned to the U.S., our American teammates were anxious to hear about all the things we had experienced. Relying on the steno pad I used as a journal, I started telling them about the different things we had done. Someone noticed that at different breaks in my notes, there were lists and asked me about them. Embarrassed, I told them that I had asked about <u>everything</u> I could think of. I had asked the missionaries how much their electricity and water bills were, how much they paid for fuel, what stuff was available at the market, what wasn't and how much those things cost, too. Much to my surprise, they asked me for a copy! When I asked why they were interested in my lists, they said it had been years since they have been to Africa. My journal was an up-to-date record of day-to-day expenses for us to live there and it was specific for Sotik, the city we were moving to. It was hard for me to believe that my nosiness would be used to our advantage. They said it would be useful as a guide to know how much monthly support to raise and to decide on what items to take and what to leave behind.

While we were getting things underway in the US, our 'new' teammates were doing their part to help us get to Kenya. They were looking around their towns trying to find us houses that had electricity and running water. Not as easy a task as it may sound! The Chowning's landlord was quite an entrepreneur. He had as many businesses as he had wives to manage them for him. When he heard there were *wazungu* trying to find not only one, but three houses, he quickly fenced in one of his many pastures and built the houses for us. (Richard Chowning signed the contracts on our behalf so construction could get underway, in the hope that the houses would be ready when our team got there.)

Our house—notice the homemade ladders under windows

Cyndi, Richard's wife, kindly sent us copies of the floor plans as soon as she got them. These plans had the measurements of the windows and of the rooms which helped us to decide on furnishings. Cyndi also measured the vacant 'Van Rheenen House', which was going to be used by the Kehls, so we could all be working on plans for our future homes together. Those measurements enabled us to buy the material in the States where the quality of fabric and selection was better. In this one area, I was well equipped because I had sewn from an early age in my mother's drapery shop, which she operated from our home. After college I worked in different aspects of the interior design business, from consultation work in a department store to curtain installation in a high-end design shop that decorated Southern plantations. I was happy to finally use one of my talents for the team's benefit. When I shared with the ladies about the variety of fabric shops in Memphis, one of our team meetings was held there so we all could go fabric shopping together since I knew how to calculate yardage.

Our four families decided to share a 20'x 8'x 8' container, making each family's portion 5'x 8'x 8'. Along with the fabrics we had purchased, we packed electric sewing machines and other sewing notions into the container. We crammed as much as we could into that little space. If one of us thought of something that we thought would be helpful, we shared that information with the others. We put in American appliances— washers, refrigerators, microwaves, typewriters, a computer, a TV and video player and lots of electrical step-down trans- formers to run all of them. When the current Sotik team asked if we could put in a lawn mower for them, we put one in for our team, too. We brought American non-perishable foods and seasonings, pictures, photo albums, knick-knacks, sheets, blankets, towels, Tupperware®, Corelle®, pots and pans. Whatever we thought could travel across the ocean in our container and help us with our transition into our new homes in Kenya, we packed it! On the day we packed the container, we were surprised when there was still some empty space. It was better to ship the container as full as possible to keep things from shifting around. So at the last minute, we planned for the future and ran out and bought baby beds, car seats and cribs.

Even though our team planned to leave the United States together to begin our work in Kenya, we wound up leaving at different times. That was because each family unit needing to raise financial support for salaries, to raise money for a new 4WD truck and to spend time with their congregations, all finished up at different times. Daryl and I were the last family to leave. We were being delayed because we were having trouble raising the large amount needed for a new truck. (There was a high import duty tax charged on all new vehicles that came into Kenya). Anxious to join our teammates, our elders suggested we go with the money we had and try to purchase a used truck in Kenya instead of waiting until we had enough money to purchase a new one. With that decision made we were ready to say farewell to our supporting congregation, have our tearful goodbyes with our families and loved ones and begin our new life in Kenya.

Our new teammates picked us up at the airport, that time. Going to the guest house where we were staying while in Nairobi, we dropped off our bags. And, just like before on our survey trip, we accompanied them on errands instead of sleeping like we so much wanted to do. After I while, when they noticed we were not really paying much attention, they suggested that we purchase some things since we were in Nairobi where the selection was better. Now excited instead of sleepy, we looked at things around us with interest. At their suggestion, Daryl picked out a shovel, a hoe and a *panga*— machete for use in the garden and yard. I picked out a couple of woven shopping baskets and *kangas*. There was no luxury of paper or plastic bags at that time. You bought it; you brought your own bag to carry it.

Kangas were used for everything imaginable. You wrapped it around your dress to protect it as you worked out in the field and around the house, much like we would an apron. You secured your child to your back like we would use an infant carrier. You spread it on the ground like a blanket or used it as a cape or shawl against the cold. They were very handy to have around. That one piece of cloth took the place of many objects that we in America would use. They are so versatile a book was written about them called, <u>Kangas: 101 Uses</u>.

After picking out these things, I began to feel a bit more confident. That was until my teammate, Kathy Rogers, suggested I buy some pre-packaged food items because they were cheaper in Nairobi and you could buy in bulk there, too. Now I was back to feeling overwhelmed again. All recipes and menus went right out of my head. When I asked her what kinds of things could be made here, she responded with, "Whatever you want. You just have to make it from scratch!"

I must have still looked bewildered because she showed me the things on her shopping list and explained the meals she was going to prepare with them. Feeling a little less disconcerted, I started looking at the things on the shelves with a different eye but I did not recognize any of the brands. I soon realized it didn't really matter what I bought, because there was only one or two choices of any given product and most of those were the Kenylon® brand, a Kenyan manufacturing company.

In 1987, when we arrived in Kenya, there was a ban on imported products in place. Pre-packaged foods were limited, prices were high and quality was poor. The ban was lifted four years later and things changed drastically. In fact, we sporadically got shipments of Dr. Pepper® in a can

(some-times with the old pull tab tops), Snickers® candy bars and Doritos® chips. It was fun to see 'Made in the USA' printed on them. Those items were so out of the ordinary to us that we gave them as gifts to each other. They found their way into our stockings at Christmas, too. We will sometimes put them in our stockings here in the US, even though they are readily avail-able, as a special remembrance of that time.

The next day, as we drove around the city again, I remarked on how beautiful all the plants and flowers were. When we went on our survey trip, it was in the month of June during Kenya's 'wintertime'. Although very green at that time of year, there didn't seem to be the profusion of flowers that were occurring now, in October, which is their 'springtime'. Kenya doesn't have four true seasons as we are used to seasons in America. It is beautifully green year-round. Even though Kenya is on the equator, large portions of it are on a mountainous plateau with elevations of a mile or more; which allows the temperatures and climates to be ideal. At the lower elevations, in the desert regions and on the coast, the heat can become unbearable. But, in Nairobi where the elevation is around 4,600 feet and springtime, the vistas are remarkable.

Our comments about the loveliness of our surroundings reminded them to tell us about our houses. They were built on what had once been a pasture, so the yards were pretty bare. They told us we should probably buy any plants we liked that were for sale because like everything else, there was more variety and better prices in Nairobi. This turned out to be a well-timed conversation because within minutes we were approached by a young man while we sat in traffic. He walked up to the truck, holding a beautiful red flower up to our window with fresh dirt dangling from its roots. (It looked as if he had just ripped it out of someone's lawn, which he actually might have done.) He asked if we wanted to buy it. We asked the Rogers if that was okay and they assured us that it was. Since we both liked it, we agreed on the price and bought the other two he had; all before the traffic started up again. The flower we purchased that day was an amaryllis. We liked them so much; we wound up digging them up and taking them with us whenever we moved.

As we traveled to Sotik, we continued the conversation about the houses and found out that even though the Rogers were in their house, the other two houses were still not finished, but very close to being so. The Vicks, along with their one year old son, Josiah, were renting a tiny, cement, hut-shaped house in town that had electricity and running water while they were waiting for their house to be finished. The Rogers, kindly invited us to stay with them until our house was finished.

Even though it was dark when we arrived; we borrowed a flashlight to look at our new house. This was the first true 'house' we ever had. We had lived in apartments, mainly student housing, up until that time. In the dark it looked pretty good. However, the next morning, by the light of day, we saw exactly where we stood. There was more undone than we realized. Still, it seemed to us that it shouldn't take much longer. After a couple of weeks, when we saw how slowly the work was progressing, we decided to ready one room in the house and move into it; ready or not.

One morning shortly after we moved in, we asked when the bathroom would be finished. The workman looked at us strangely and said; "It *is* finished."

Daryl and I looked at each other, and then looked at the bathroom to see what he called 'finished'. The room was tiled, but the grout was smeared everywhere. The windowpanes were in, but the paint was splashed all over the glass. The sink was in, but it was held up by pipes sticking out of the wall. There was a shower fixture running up the side of the wall with only a drain beneath it, but no shower stall. We learned this was an European-style bathroom. We were supposed to walk into the bathroom, closing the door behind us and take a shower in the room with everything getting wet. On this point we chose to fall back to our American ways and asked them to build us a shower stall. We they didn't seem to understand what we meant, we drew up a plan using the drain in the floor as a guide to decide the measurements. Our 'shower' was built out of plywood with a short cement and plaster footing to contain the water and to attach the plywood to. When it was finished, Daryl gave the plywood several coats of paint and I made a shower curtain. (Hearing what we had done, our teammates came by to take a look. They had the builders do the same thing at their houses, while the workers were still available.)

It was interesting to watch people build a house with just hand tools and no power tools. To us, this was hard to imagine! My siblings and I had helped our parents build a house and then to restore and remodel an old Victorian one, but we used all kinds of power tools to do it. Another interesting aspect of Kenyan construction was the clean-up process. It would have frazzled my mom's nerves because there seemed to be none. Everything just got thrown onto the floor or out the window. I must admit it was a little unnerving to me, too. As we looked at our 'home' with fresh eyes, we saw there was a lot of work to be done before we could find 'homes' for all of our things. Making a list of jobs to be done, we divvied up the work between the two of us. Even our little amaryllis bulbs had to wait to be planted because there was so much construction trash all around the edge of the house and in the yard. That area, too, would need a good picking-up, raking and fertilizing before it would be good enough for any type of plants.

The next day, Daryl worked on the outside while I tackled the floors. As I swept our cement floors in the living room for the *third* time, I finally saw its true color. It was not the deep maroon color of Kathy's floor it was a pale, swirling pink. When I asked her about this, she explained that in Kenya, a powder was put into the cement as it was mixed to help keep mold from coming up through the floor. (Since it was an expensive product, the builder probably used the amount that should have been used for one house for all three houses. Dividing the powder between our houses, made the floors this pink swirling color and not very effective.)

This will be our living room which has cement floors

Now, in order to keep the mold from growing, I needed to apply several coats of a red oxide paste to the floors. Each of these coats had to be rubbed in *by hand* and left to dry; then buffed *by hand* before the next coat was put on. This process culminated with a final clear top coat of wax paste that was also to be buffed *by hand* with special sheepskins until it was shiny. My modest sized house now took on gargantuan proportions as I envisioned all the work ahead of me.

ALL the floors needed to be swept several times to get up all the dirt and residue and then mopped several times before I could even begin to put on the multiple coats of wax. I was so overwhelmed, I felt like crying! So, I decided I would forego this delightful and labor intensive task until there were fewer workers tramping dirt and mud into the house on a regular basis. (After all, it was still under construction.) I decided I would sweep daily and maybe even mop on occasion until I absolutely HAD to put the wax on. I now looked at the other chores on our 'to-do-list' fondly. In comparison, they seemed like a walk in the park!

A short time later, I realized I couldn't put off the dreaded waxing much longer and began cleaning the floors. As I did so a man with graying hair and stretched out earlobes, which he had tucked onto the top of his ears, knocked on the door. He greeted me with the customary, *"Ochamage?*—How are you?"(Literally, is everything in agreement?)

I responded in kind with, *"Ee, mising*—yes, very well."

Thinking I knew Kalenjin because I returned his greeting in the proper manner, he continued speaking to me in Kalenjin. (I was laboriously learning this language but my husband seemed to be soaking it up like a sponge.) Having just about exhausted what little of the language I had learned, I just stood there until he realized I didn't know what he was saying. About that time, Daryl came inside and the greetings started again; along with the prepared speech he must have just given me. But this time, he shyly handed Daryl a letter as he spoke.

Showing me that the letter was typed in English, I read the letter along with Daryl and soon realized it was a letter of reference. It was a glowing letter about what a great 'boy' Kipsang Joseph Mursi was. That British idiom began to irritate me until I glanced up at the date and saw it was written in the '60s. This pristine letter had been written when he *was* a boy, or a young man, and during the time that Kenya was still a British colony. The letter had been carefully stored and used over the years for occasions just such as this one, almost twenty five years later, when he would need a reference.

I was shocked and didn't know what to do when I finally realized what he was asking of us. He had heard that there were *wazungu* in the area and had come to apply for the job of housekeeper. Not knowing how to respond to this, we went down to Kathy and Eddie's house to ask them what they thought. It all boiled down to whether we were ready or not to have someone work in our house. We knew that we were expected to hire people to work for us because unemployment was so high. Most people had someone who tended the food garden, lawn and other jobs that were considered 'outside' jobs and another person on the 'inside' who helped with all the tedious day-to-day chores of running a house. They suggested we hire him on a trial basis. That way, if things didn't work out, we could just let him go.

The employee/employer business was new to us. Daryl and I quietly discussed what we could have him do on the in-side of the house. Everything we thought of seemed premature because we were not truly 'running the house' yet. We figured once the floors were done we would be able to hire him....THE FLOORS!!...How could I have forgotten about them? If he didn't work out for us, at least the floors got done. If he did work out well with us, the floors still got done! It seemed like a win-win situation all the way around. With the Rogers help, we decided on the hours to be worked and the salary. We all concluded the negotiations in good spirits because our dreaded floors would get cleaned and waxed and Kipsang got the housekeeping job he applied for.

He did an excellent job and worked for us the whole time we lived in the little country town of Sotik. Kipsang was such a blessing to me. Before I had learned enough Kalenjin, I panto-mimed the things I wanted him to do. I'm sure he laughed on his way home and retold the stories around the fire at night to his wife and children about the crazy things that *mzungu* lady did that day. If the roles were reversed, I'm sure I would have done the same thing myself.

As we continued to settle into our new life in Africa, Daryl and I sat around by the glow of a kerosene lamp or by candlelight in the evenings. We liked to talk about the different things that happened during the day while we ate supper. Without the distraction of electricity, we spent a lot more time together that first year. Our lives had been so hectic in America with school, working, fundraising and preparing for missions that it was nice to have this slower pace of life for a time. It also helped us to get reconnected with each other so that we would be able to face the trials that were ahead.

LESSON LEARNED

I never cease to be amazed at the way in which
God chooses to answer prayers. Sometimes
He will even send the answer right to your door!

Kipsang Joseph Arap Mursi

SIX

lo

(lo)

"Uh, oh…your well is dried up."

"Oh thank goodness I thought it was serious.
Well, can you fill it up? There's a hose out back."
Movie: Baby Boom

DRINKING WATER
TAKES HOURS

Our house, which had a typical American floor plan, wasn't built in the usual American way. Rocks approximately nine inches by one to two feet long were hacked out of a mountainside quarry miles away and brought by truck to our location. These rocks were then stacked and mortared together to form the walls. After the walls were finished, lines were chiseled out for the electrical components and some of the water pipes. Once the doors, windows, plumbing, and electrical components were in place, the house was smeared inside and out with a cement plaster. The outside was left rough like stucco, but the inside was made as smooth as sheet rock. But, unlike sheet rock, the plaster veneer crumbled easily whenever you hammered in a nail to hang something. As a result, we hung things with a lot of forethought and care. The layout of our houses' floor plans included three bedrooms, two bathrooms (one with a bathtub and the other with the shower stall we designed), a living room, a dining room and a kitchen with a walk-in pantry, all on a small scale.

Our houses being built by hand, no power tools

The water ran, most of the time. A single phone line was installed in our bedroom (five months after we moved to Kenya) powered by a large car battery because we had no electricity. Even though the house was wired for electricity, we did not actually have the transformer to run it until seven months after we moved in. Whenever we asked when it would be turned on, we always got the same answer. "It is coming. It will be here next week."

But I tried not to complain. I felt very blessed to have what we had. Most Africans live in an adobe-like mud hut that has a thatched roof, without either running water or electricity and certainly no phones. During the '80s and '90s when we lived there, we saw them do without these things on a daily basis and it gave me a deeper appreciation for phones, running water and electricity when I had them. Granted we had shortages or rationing of all of these items the entire time we lived in Kenya. But, whenever I had all of them in abundance and at the same time, it felt like a luxury.

As we began housekeeping 'Kenya-style', we learned how to do without many things, including electricity. You may think, *"How can you live without electricity?"* But, when you live in a country where it's the minority that have electricity and the majority that don't, it was not as difficult to accomplish. Kerosene, petrol, propane gas tanks and batteries of all kinds were used in the place of the power that electricity provided and could be purchased at gas or 'petrol' stations. Propane tanks varied in size from the average two feet tall to about five feet tall. It is the same type of tank that we in America use on our outside grills. We hooked up those propane tanks to our stove, refrigerator, freezer, etc. in much the same way you would to your grill. For a short time, we shared a small dorm-size refrigerator that our teammates, Dave and Brenda Vick, were using.

However, our electrical problems were abated for a while when the Chowning family moved back to America. We made the team decision to continue renting the Chowning's house and to split the cost four ways. By renting that space, it allowed the men to have office space away from their homes. (Sermon and lesson prep were made even more laborious because they needed to be taught in Kalenjin. So, having a quiet place to concentrate where they wouldn't be disturbed became very important.) The house also gave the ladies a place to set up our refrigerators, sewing machines and many of the other electrical items we had grown up using. The task of sewing curtains and creating other items for our homes was now more convenient to accomplish with the aid of electricity and those machines. Instead of preparing small meals every time we ate, we could now make casseroles and the leftovers could be refrigerated or frozen for another meal. Sodas, milk and juices were kept chilled, hard to find packaged meats could now be bought and frozen. But, best of all—ICE was now available to put it in our tea and whatever else we wanted to drink. No more room temperature drinks! We did have to walk the equivalent of a block or more to get to the Chownings' house, but the convenience it provided made it worth the effort.

At first I thought renting the Chowning's house was extravagant. *"Shouldn't we just be patient and wait for the electricty to be connected? They said it would come any day now."* Later, I was so thankful for the 'splurge' because it took seven months before we actually got the electricity hooked up. (Incredibly, there was a debate between the power company, the landlord and us, over who would purchase the power transformer so that our three houses could be supplied with electricity. When Eddie, on the teams behalf, said we would no longer pay rent until we got the electricity we were promised in our contract, the debate was soon settled. Our landlord paid for the electical transformer, not the power company!)

One day without warning, a man knocked on our door wearing a tool belt. We couldn't believe it when he said he was there to hook up our electricity. While he went from house to house making sure everything was in proper working order, a flatbed truck carrying the transformer stopped in the field in front of our houses. With the aid of several men, the transformer was raised and attached to a pole. Cables were then attached from it to our houses. Brenda Vick, the only one of us with a baby at that time, cried. She had been handwashing Josiah's cloth diapers and now she could start using the washing machine. All of us got a kick out of walking around the house turning on switches only to realize we needed to run out and buy light bulbs! Many things became easier when we finally got our electricity, but going without electricity had its merits, too. For only seven months we felt what most of the world feels everyday; what it is like to do without electricity.

Kipsang assisting electrician to hook up power to house

Sotik is situated 3° from the Equator and at an elevation of around 6000 feet. Being so close to the equator gives little variance to sunrise and sunset. It daily occurs between 6 to 7 o'clock, both a.m. and p.m., year round. Because of this, we became like the farmers we were surrounded by; up with the rooster and to bed by around 9 p.m. When you had to do whatever you wanted to do by candlelight, kerosene light or flashlight, you got tired and sometimes frustrated pretty quickly because you couldn't see what you were doing very well. Also, living at this higher elevation made your body work harder, without you even realizing it. The air had less oxygen in it then we were accustomed to and consequently required us to need more sleep. Altering our sleeping patterns was just one more thing we needed to change in order to better adapt to our new environment. Living in Kenya affected just about every area of our lives; communication, sleep, food and even the water we drank. You can not drink water directly from the tap/faucet in Kenya because the water is not treated. We could wash with it, cook with it, bathe in it, brush our teeth with it but not drink it. Some of the first purchases we made were a gas operated stove, a counter top water filtration system and a big five gallon *sufaria*—cooking pot so that we could make our own clean, uncontaminated water to drink.

This was the process we followed every day for clean water. Filled up the *sufaria* and lit the gas burner with a match. Sounds easy enough, but the matches didn't always light the first time. Typically, we would have a little pile of five to ten matchsticks that had fizzled out and not made a flame. One brand was even ironically called 'Lucky Strike'. We jokingly said it meant, 'you're lucky *if* they strike,' so we tried to avoid getting those. My favorite brand of matches was called, Zebra, which had a zebra playfully kicking up its heels on its cover. I liked those because they were made out of wax-coated paper and seemed to catch every time.

After lighting the burner, we would then heave the pot of water onto the burner and cover it with it's flat, handleless lid that looked more like a pizza pan. The water was then boiled to kill any water borne diseases. (Drinking untreated water can cause 'travelers' diarhea'.) And I'm here to say that old adage is true; 'A watched pot doesn't boil!' Or, that's the way it seemed because it took more time to boil liquids at high altitudes. (The next time you pick up a pre-packaged food item, notice the adjustments given for cooking at high altitudes.) Once the water finally came to a boil, we would set our kitchen timers for the required twenty minutes so we wouldn't forget about it. From the time the water was first put on to boil until the timer went off, it took over an hour. Then the water would need to sit for a time to cool down. When the water was too hot, the large five gallon sufaria was hard to handle and it could also crack the candles in the water fitration system.

The system was two five-gallon enamel covered steel cans that stacked one on top of the other like double-boilers. The lower can had a faucet-type dispenser on it to easily obtain the water. The upper can had holes in the bottom of it, into which you screwed in baked clay 'candles'. These candles allowed the water to flow through, but kept the dirt and other undesireables out. The condition of the candles was very important. When you first purchased them, you needed to soak them in bleach water to remove the chalky residue. If you didn't, the water tasted awful and you would have to pour it out—wasting both your time and cooking gas.

We would take the filtration system apart weekly in order to remove any residue that might have accumulated and to check the candles for cracks. After everything was taken apart and inspected, it was given a good scrub with the brush that was provided with it at the time of purchase. (It reminded me of a nail buffer.) With the candles out of the way, you could easily wash out the canisters with previously filtered water and then reassemble. Imagine, all of that work, just for drinkable water! After doing this day in and day out, it seemed almost decadent when we returned to the United States and were able to just put a glass up to the faucet to get a drink of water. What a blessing, that so many people take for granted. No hauling, no boiling, no filtering—just *clean*, running, drinkable water!

Another problem with the water not being treated was that sometimes your water looked like weak tea. But at times the desire for a long, warm soak in the tub helped you to ignore the dirty appearance of the bath water. During times of drought and/or low rainfall, the darker water was more easily visible. Be that as it may, I would still be amazed at the fine 'mud' silt that I could skim off of the candles when I cleaned them. Despite the condition of the the water, running water was running water. Water, regardless of how dirty, was more desirable coming out of my faucet, than having to perform the back breaking job of carrying it up from the river. Even with 'running' water there were still times when we had water shortages. We soon learned to adopt the practice of the locals by putting simple gutters on the house to channel the rain from our corrugated tin roof into fifty-five gallon drums to collect water when it rained. When the water was 'on' we kept the drums filled up with the water hose in anticipation of it going off again, which it always did, sooner or later.

One morning before we realized that water wasn't always available, we began our morning using water in the normal manner. I went into the kitchen to fill the sufaria to begin processing the water, but the water wouldn't come out of the cold water faucet. Water came out of the hot water faucet, but I didn't want to use it since Daryl was taking a shower. I knew the water worked in the bathroom, so I filled the pan from the faucet on the bathtub. Explaining this oddity to Daryl when he came into the kitchen, he thought maybe we had an airlock in the pipe. Not much later, one of our teammates came by to say they were having problems with their water. He was checking to see if we were, too.

"We have water everywhere but in one of the kitchen faucets." I told him.

"Oh. Then the water must be off." He responded.

"But we have water." I said in a confused tone, showing him what I was talking about. He explained that the cold water tap was the main supply line into the house and that all the other pipes in the house drew their water from the storage tank up in the attic.

"We have a storage tank in the attic?" I asked.

"Yes, we all do. When the water is 'on' it keeps the tank filled up. Then when water is needed, gravity pulls it down from the attic to wherever you turn on a faucet or flush a toilet." After that he added, "You'd better start conserving water until it comes back on again. We don't know when that will be. I better get home and tell them the water's off."

Water filter →

Setting up the kitchen
I'm peeling plastic off a new stove that is hooked up to a propane gas tank.

To my right by the sink are glass kerosene lamps we used the entire time we lived in Kenya. To my left is a large walk-in pantry which also housed the washing machine

After he left, Daryl climbed up into the attic to inspect our tank. Being a reserve tank it only held about a hundred gallons of water and it was almost empty. He yelled down for us not to use any more water. Kipsang, who had now reported for work, was watching all of this with interest. We patted the faucet and shook our heads trying to communicate not to use it. Feeling we weren't explaining the situation properly, I went down to the Rogers and asked them if their worker could come up to our house and explain what was going on to our workers.

By this time, we had also hired Joseph Ng'eno to work on the outside of the house doing lawn and garden care. Joseph cared for the individual grass plugs we had planted in the hopes for a lawn. He nurtured and trimmed the hedge on our part of the compound, which we had put in for protection and privacy. When we first purchased the trees, they were about the thickness of a pencil and about one to two feet tall. I thought it would take ten to twenty years before they would do us any good. But, like most foliage in Kenya, it grew like a weed and within a couple of years; we had a nice, thick, tall hedge.

Joseph maintained our section of the vegetable garden. He pruned the flower beds around the yard and groomed the fruit and the decorative trees we had also selected and that he had planted. Since we had no power tools, this was a big tedious job to be done by hand. Even so, Joseph took pride in his work and made our yard look lovely. With our consent, he took cuttings from our lawn and planted them on his own compound. It was fun whenever we would go to visit him and saw the contrast of the fineness of the roses, lilies and other flowers against the rusticness of the mud hut. Inside, he would have those same flowers arranged in glass vases. The 'vases' were actually chipped soda bottles (now non-returnable) and/or chipped glass jars he had rescued from our trash pit. Joseph and Kipsang would always have an eye out for things that I had thrown out after it was empty, chipped or had lost its lid.

I didn't have any more use for it, but they would take it home and reuse for a new purpose. Developing nations have a lot to teach other countries about recycling.

With the help of the Rogers' worker, the water situation was explained to our workers and everyone nodded in understanding. Kipsang walked over to the kitchen faucet and patted it in mimicry, shaking his head with a big grin on his face to show he understood. Thankfully, that time, the water was back on before the end of the day. There were other times that the water was off for days and occasionally weeks. We became used to the sound of the water coming back on in the middle of the night to fill the upstairs tank. We would give a contented sigh and roll over unless the sound was also accompanied by a splashing noise. This meant a faucet had been left on and now that the water was back, it was running down the drain instead of going up the pipes into the reserve tank. Or, the overflow valve was clogged in the attic tank and now the water was pouring onto the ceiling above our heads. Either way, someone needed to get up and take care of the splashing sound. If the sound came from overhead, Daryl usually took care of it. If it was the noise of a splashing faucet, I took care of it.

On one occasion, the water was off for an extended period and Daryl was out of town. If he had been there he would have performed the laborious task of putting water in our reserve tank in the attic. This was done by filling the jerry cans from the 55-gallon drums outside, dragging them into the hallway below the opening to the attic, tying a rope to the handle and then hauling them up into the attic to dump the contents into the reserve tank. (We learned after that first time the water went off, to always keep water stored in reserve in jerry cans and in the 55-gallon drums.) By filling the reserve tank in this manner, we could still take hot showers because the gravity fed hot water heater pulled its water from the reserve tank. But this stretch of no water had depleted the drums and I was miserly hoarding the last of our water for cooking and drinking (even though I really wanted to wash my hair).

Kipsang and Joseph standing on the lawn and in front of the hedge that were both put in by hand after we moved to Kenya

On this particular morning when I woke up and went into the kitchen to prepare breakfast, there was a huge puddle of water, about five feet wide and half an inch thick at its deepest point, under the dining room table (the lowest point in the room). I skirted around the puddle and walked to the sink, there to see it overflowing with the stopper in the drain. I jerked the stopper out in exasperation. As it was draining, I started turning the faucets off and on. Nothing happened. It was then that I realized the water had come on, run for a while and then gone off again. I was so tired; I had slept through it all! Quickly, I put the stopper back in place, but there wasn't much left by that point. I felt like crying. All that lovely water wasted!

Turning my back on the sink, I stood there seriously contemplating if there was enough water in the puddle on the floor under the table for me to roll around in to wash my hair. Who knows what would have happened if Kipsang had not come into the house about that time. He took it all in, turning the faucets like I had. Then with a tsk, tsk and a shake of his head, he grabbed a mop and started clearing up the puddle. I'm ashamed to say that I was so disappointed that I left him to clean it up while I went into the bedroom to have a little cry.

Being on a higher incline on the hillside than our team-mates' houses, our water always went 'off' first and came back 'on' last. Because of this, Daryl worked it out with Joseph and Kipsang to keep the reserve tank in the attic filled in his absence. Kipsang filled the jerry cans from the drums outside and carried them down the hallway, stopping underneath the opening to the attic. Joseph, up in the attic, would have a rope dangling down from the opening. Kipsang would tie this around the handle so Joseph could haul it up and then, dump the water into the reserve tank.

Another time years later, we were having another long stretch without water or rain. An unexpected rainstorm hit in the middle of the night. The rain quickly filled our barrels, which had previously been bone dry. As luck would have it, Daryl was out of town again. (I don't know why those things seemed to happen when he was gone.) I was pregnant with our second child, Steven and Lydia was still in cloth diapers. Jumping out of bed, I threw a hooded raincoat on over my nightgown and pulled on a pair of rubber boots. Grabbing a plastic bucket from the pantry, I ran outside into the pouring rain, thankful there was no thunder or lightning.

After shoving the bucket into the drum to get water, I carried the bucket into the house and dumped the water into the bathtub to try to collect as much water as I could since I had no idea how long the rain would last. I lost count of how many trips I made back and forth between the drum and the bathtub. At one point, I had to stop to throw towels on the floor from the back door to the bathtub because the floor was getting slippery. As I was lifting out another bucket, Eddie showed up. He knew that Daryl was out of town and that we, like they, were desperate for the water. I think he was just as surprised to see me as I was to see him. We looked at each other for a few stunned seconds.

Grinning, I said the one word that would make sense out of what I was doing out in the middle of the night in the pouring rain: "Diapers."

He smiled and nodded his head. We all had children in cloth diapers at that time and we all needed and were longing to wash those diapers. He fussed at me for lugging the heavy pail because I was pregnant. When I showed him the bucket was only half-full, he let me continue to help him. With Eddie using the five-gallon jerry cans, the tub was quickly filled. With that done, he asked, "Have you filled the washing machine?"

"Oh! I never even thought to do that!" I exclaimed.

So we worked together and quickly got that filled, too. The rain was still coming down, but after Eddie filled all of our jerry cans, there was nothing left to fill. I thanked him for his help and he went back to his house. I never asked him if he thought to come out on his own or if Kathy had asked him to do it. Either way, I was extremely thankful for his thoughtfulness.

After he left, the rain was still coming down, but at a gentler pace. Since I was wide awake from the middle of the night exertions, I decided to start washing as many things as I could while the rain held out. The first things to be washed were the cloth diapers because they were so rank! I think I washed about three or four loads that night before the rain finally stopped. With the reserve tank empty, the washing machine had to be filled by bucket for each of the wash and rinse cycles. If Eddie had seen me dumping all those buckets of water in the washing machine, he really would have had reason to fuss at me like he had earlier.

In contrast to the pouring rain of the night before, the next morning brought brilliant sunshine. It was funny to see all of our clotheslines filled to overflowing with clothes and cloth diapers. When I saw that Brenda had strung up some extra clothesline, I dug around and found some rope so Joseph could do the same for us. But before everything had time to finish drying, another light ran came. When Daryl got home later that day, I had clothes draped on every surface I could think of trying to get them to dry. I even pinned the cloth diapers together at the corners and circled the hot water heater with them when I ran out of furniture to drape the clothes onto. Necessity certainly is the mother of invention, because I found this to be a very effective way to dry diapers and other small items. I wound up using this technique the rest of the time we were there when it rained or when I needed something to be washed and dried quickly.

After we first arrived in Sotik and found that our brand new houses didn't have electricity, I did wonder how we would manage. But, we soon learned ways to get around not having electricity. Most of the people in the world live without electricity every day. When you have substitutes you can use in place of electricity, it's not that difficult to live without. But what I soon learned was **no one** can live without water.

LESSON LEARNED

Things we think of as necessities often turn into luxuries after being seen through the eyes of poverty and experience.

Our daughter Lydia, out visiting I the village, sitting on a 55-gallon drum used to store water

seven

tisab
(tis ahb)

"And you never know who God is gonna use,
a princess or a baby; maybe even you or me."
Song: "<u>Who God is Gonna Use</u>" by Rich Mullins

CULTURE GOES
A LONG WAY

As our team became more established, we tried to soak in as much of the local culture as we could. Given that college was in our not too distant past, we decided to approach our study of the Kipsigis culture in much the same manner as we would a class. We decided to hold a 'cultural seminar' and gave each other time to choose and research topics. These studies proved to be very informative. In tackling the culture in that manner, it immersed us in a way like none other. By pooling our information, it enabled us to learn a lot in a short period of time. The subjects we chose to study were the educational system, modern medical care, tropical diseases, the allure of the witch doctor, drunkenness and the rites of passage.

Dave and Brenda Vick chose to study the educational system. This covered things like: the age children began school, how they tested to see if a child was ready for school, the subjects taught, discipline in the classroom, the level of education the average child achieved, the part school uniforms played and the cost of education. They shared that education was not free. If you wanted your children to be educated, you had to pay school fees and buy school uniforms. Poor families, who couldn't afford to send all their children, had to make the decision as to which of their children would be educated and which would not. Most often when a choice had to be made, the boys were chosen because they would one day be the providers for their families. More than likely, these boys turned to men, would work away from home where English and a good education would be very important.

The Vicks also found out that the community built the schools, not the government. The land was given to the community to build on and a water pipe would be brought to the site, but that was about it. Since the communities were poor, these school buildings were usually simple wooden structures with dirt floors. Children were not provided with textbooks to take home for their own use. Any books they did have were shared. School supplies were minimal. Meals were not provided and their 'bathroom' was a drop latrine. Students were expected to pay attention in class. If they didn't, or if they came to school late or caused any kind of trouble, they received a whack on the hand as punishment.

There was no electricity. Openings were strategically spaced along the walls in lieu of windows to allow for cross-ventilation. If it rained, the openings or 'windows' could be closed up with simple wooden shutters. Since these were the communities' buildings, they were also used as churches on the weekends. When used for evening meetings in the area, a kerosene lamp was hung from the rafters. These conditions sound rather harsh to Americans, but this is how the average Kenyan lived so they felt they had provided a respectable school for the children in their area.

Just as the building was simple, the way to check to see if a child was ready to attend school was simple, too. The child must be able to stretch an arm up over his head and touch the opposite ear. When we first heard this we thought it was a strange African custom. But then Brenda, who had studied child development in college, explained that a child does not have the physical and mental coordination to be able to do this simple act until they are around five or six years old! Now instead of thinking the test was strange, we thought it was very clever or, 'spot on' to use a British phrase. (This type of thing happened a lot—to me, anyway. Something that at first seemed rather backwards would later make perfect sense and instead seemed very astute!)

Since Susan Kehl and Kathy Rogers, were both nurses, they looked into the local medical facilities and their practices. They found out many interesting facts about tropical diseases and medical conditions specific to our area and how to treat them. For some reason, Kenyans do not seem to suffer from appendicitis the way Americans do. What Kenyans do have problems with is their uvula (the little punching bag hanging down at the back of your throat). Their uvulas could continue to grow down into their throats until they needed to have an uvulaectomy in much the same manner we have a tonsilectomy. Kenyans also do not have the Rh incompatibility factor to contend with that Americans have. Fielden once had to drive to several different cities to find the medicine for Janet because the facility they used simply did not carry it. He was racing against the seventy-two hour window after the birth of their child to find it and made it with not much time to spare.

Susan and Kathy also researched and explained about the allure of the witch doctor and things the clinics had to do to combat this. They said that even if the clinic could not find anything wrong with the patient, they would give them a vitamin shot instead of sending them home with nothing. The health care workers at the hospital said that if they didn't give them an injection or some sort of medicine, they would seek a 'cure' from the witch doctor. So, in order to keep them coming back to the clinic or hospital, they gave them vitamin shots. The injection didn't harm them; it usually made them feel better and made them more likely to repeat the process when the clinic or hospital was really needed. Eddie, the only one on our team who brought over a computer and printer, typed up the paper and gave us each a copy as his contribution to the study. (Since this was in '88, just prior to the computer explosion that was about to take place, the rest of us just wrote our reports by hand and read them out loud.)

With drunkenness rampant in the Kipsigis culture, Kevin Kehl decided to study about the manufacture and selling of the local home-brewed alcohol called *maiywek*. At times this brew was lethal because it had such a high 'proof' content and could be made of some fairly toxic ingredients. He explained that with unemployment being so high, some people turned to alcohol to try to numb their feelings of inadequacy because they couldn't provide for their families. It was not an uncommon sight to see a man passed out along the side of the road or staggering around in town or down the road. However, it was unusual to see women like this. That didn't mean that they didn't drink or that they didn't contribute to alcoholism. They were just more private about it. Years later, this helped us to better understand the testimony of one of our new Christians who had been abandoned by her husband. Esther found providing alcohol for the village an easy, lucrative way to make money. She showed us the slight dip in the center of her hut where the communal beer pot sat. Men sat, circled around this large clay pot, and drank from it with long bamboo 'straws', about four feet long, that had a woven filter on the end. Later, when she became a Christian, she stopped selling *maiywek* and put in a small *kiosk*—store. It was not as profitable, but she had great pride in the fact that she did not have to rely on *maiywek* for money and that she no longer aided in the drunkenness of her village.

Esther's hut, used for Bible study instead of 'homebrew'

Daryl and I decided to cover the four 'rites of passage'. These four rites are: birth, adulthood, marriage and death.

Through discussions at church and later with Antony, our Kenyan co-worker, we were beginning to have more and more exposure to these subjects. These topics were so different from anything else we had ever experienced, that we wanted to find out more about them. It was difficult to get Kenyan Christians to open up and talk about these subjects because so much of it was steeped in pagan rituals and tradition. These young Christians were trying to put a lot of these 'pagan' things behind them. But when they realized we weren't condemning them, but trying to get a better understanding of their culture, they hesitantly opened up to us.

In many African cultures, including Kenya, the way to become an adult is to go through an initiation ceremony which involves a time of seclusion to impart the secrets of becoming an adult, culminating with the act of circumcision. The time of seclusion is about a month and usually takes place during the Christmas season when students have their longest school holiday. (The seasons in Kenya are the opposite of what they are in America, the warmest time of the year is at Christmas. Students have an extended time off from school at that time like we do for our summer. Our workers were also given off a month during that time as their vacation.)

Traditionally, the men are taught that their wives will be their worst enemies and that you must beat them into sub-mission. The Christian counterpart to these ceremonies was to teach Christian principals and morals to the young men. They taught them to choose their spouses wisely because if they did, they became their greatest allies, not their enemies. Also, that the better husband did not beat his wife, but instead, discussed things with her until there was a better understanding. Traditionally, to try to anesthetize the initiates for the upcoming circumcision, there is a lot of alcohol drinking going on. The alcohol was either purchased locally or homemade. To help with the pain of the circumcision, the Christian boys were taken to the hospital for a local shot of anesthesia prior to the cutting instead of getting them drunk.

So embedded is this ceremony in the culture, we sang songs about it in church. I never could understand *all* the words we sang while in church, but I usually got the gist of it. The more words I picked up, the more I enjoyed what I sang. On one occasion around circumcision time, I was hearing things that I expected: 'I won't be tempted to drink beer. I won't be tempted to steal. I won't be tempted to put curses on people.' But I listened with a sinking heart when I heard them say, "*I won't be tempted to drink soda.*"

I had begun serving soda to people who came to my door after I found out it was considered a special treat. I made sure I had a stocked case of filled soda bottles on hand for just such occasions. Plus, it was also quicker and easier to hand someone a bottle of soda than to make a pot of chaik. After services I asked Daryl why they were against sodas. He said that in an attempt to lure Christians to these 'pagan' events, they would offer them soda instead of alcohol to drink. The song was saying, 'We [Christians] won't be lured to go to the ceremonies even to just drink a soda.' That made me feel so much better. They weren't against the soda, just it being served and used as a lure to go to the circumcision ceremonies.

We also heard all kinds of stories about women and childbirth that were just as fascinating as the circumcision accounts. One of the stories that showed the differences in our cultures is this one. A very pregnant woman was walking along side the road with a group of ladies. Richard Chowning, traveling with a Kenyan man came across them on their way home from a meeting. Richard wanted to give them a ride to the hospital. But one of the older women said, no, she knew what to do. Richard watched as the old woman placed her hands on either side of the pregnant woman's mouth. Taking a deep breath, the old woman blew forcefully into the younger woman's mouth. She repeated this several times. After a bit, the pregnant woman signaled for the old lady to quit. She then walked a short distance away for a bit of privacy and had the baby. After getting her and the newborn safely home, they continued on their way. Out of curiosity, Richard asked the Kenyan man what had just transpired.

"The older woman could tell the woman in labor was having trouble, so she blew the baby out." He answered.

"Blew the baby out? You don't really think you can make a baby come out by blowing into their mouth, do you?" He said astounded that anyone could think that in this day and age.

"Well, the baby came out didn't it?" he responded, equally astounded that Richard couldn't see that that's exactly what happened.

Stories like these intrigued us even more because we discovered that I was pregnant. One morning after an episode of nausea, Kipsang became concerned for me. Thinking I had malaria, he told me I should go to the *sipitali*—hospital. I just shook my head and said, *"Mami ng'ala"* which roughly translates to—don't worry.

The nausea went on for several days, at different times throughout the day. Since Kipsang seemed so concerned about my health, I finally told him as best as I could, *"Tun awendi name lakwet*—I am going to have a baby."

He looked at me with a somewhat confused look on his face (not for the first time, I might add) and then continued with his work. Later that afternoon, our interpreter/language teacher, Antony Marusoi, came to the house for our daily lessons. Antony lived in the nearest village to Sotik and was a carpenter by trade, although his heart's work was preaching and church planting. We worked side by side all the years we lived in Sotik doing just that.

We were formally studying from a Kipsigis Grammar book, but many days we would take a break from our lessons to ask about specific words that we needed to know. At first, I wanted household words like sweep, boil, water, wash, peel, chop, etc. so I could give instructions to Kipsang who didn't speak English. Daryl wanted outside-type words for Joseph like hoe, dig, plant, stake, burn, level, cut, chop, trim, etc. for the same reason. Later on we wrote up sentences to use out in the village like, "I am learning to speak Kipsigis—*Anetege ang'alal Kipsigis.*"

That simple phrase would bring on a deluge of words, which we weren't quite ready for. So we then learned, "I don't yet hear Kipsigis very well—*Tomagas Kipsigis komie.*"

They would then smile and nod in understanding, very proud that we were trying to learn their language. When we added, *"Mutyo, mutyo—*slowly, slowly" they would patiently say words over and over or just give up all together.

But always with kindness and usually saying, *"Tun igase—*You will hear one day!"

On our tea break that particular day, I asked Antony, "How do you tell someone you are pregnant?"

He sat there with what looked like a pained smile. (We learned that this is the way Kenyans look when embarrassed.) Finally he said, "You don't say anything."

"Why not?" I asked.

"It is not spoken of in mixed company," he answered.

"Well, what if it is woman to woman?" I persisted.

"Then you say *a nyigis.*" He said.

"A nyigis," I repeated.

"What does it mean? You didn't use the word *lakwet—*baby." I continued.

"No. Why should I?" He responded. I reiterated the conversation I had earlier that morning with Kipsang. Antony smiled again, but this time in amusement and conferred in Kipsigis with him. (Kipsang always seemed to find work to do near us when we were having those lessons. I think our instruction gave him a lot of humor and helped his day to pass more quickly. Who knows, he may have been trying to pick up some English.) After talking with Kipsang, Antony asked me to repeat exactly what I had said. As I did so, both of their grins got even bigger.

"What did I say?" I asked, seeing their merriment.

"Some day I am going to take a baby. Take, as in to steal or carry it off." He answered with a big grin.(No wonder Kipsang had looked at me so strangely.)

Daryl and me in the living room with our workers
for a 'staff picture', as my sister, Carla called it.
(L to R) Kipsang, who helped us with indoor jobs,
Joseph, who helped us with outdoors jobs and
Antony, our language teacher and co-church planter

After we all had a chuckle, I glanced back at the words I'd written down. "So, *a nyigis*" I said. "What does that mean?"
"It means you are fat, heavy." He answered.

"What?" was my shocked response. "You want me to go around telling people I'm fat!?"

(Kenyans, who are normally slender, enjoyed being fat. They felt that this was a sign that you were prosperous. Americans would never dream about bragging to someone that they were fat. That was yet another example of the contrasting worldviews.)

"No. You don't tell people anything," was his calm reply

Confused, I asked, "Well, what do I say when I start missing appointments out in the village because I'm sick?"

"Just say *makaran moet*—my stomach is not good. In a few months when they see your stomach is big, they'll know you are with child," he clarified for me.

Getting back to our lesson, I thought about the things he had just said. I remembered him saying, 'being with child' and 'fat or heavy'. Those words brought to mind the old-fashioned phrase of 'being heavy with child' and gave me a better grasp of the terminology. This phrase also made me feel quite the Victorian lady and as a result, more comfortable about using it.

The next morning when Kipsang saw me after another episode of morning sickness, he patted his stomach and said, *"Makaranan moet*—Stomach not good?"

To which I hesitantly replied, *"A nygis*—I'm fat."

He broke out into a big grin, clapped his hands together in a single clap and said, *"Karanan*—good!" (Since Kipsang had six children at that time, I thought he would have figured out that my sudden onset of nausea every morning was 'morning sickness.' Maybe his wife didn't suffer from it.)

Progressing in our 'cultural seminar' studies, we were finding out that many of the 'rites' were tied to the spirit world. Children are considered a blessing in Kenya. The Kipsigis tribe saw twins as a double blessing, while other tribes saw twins as a curse. It is because of the 'spirits' that you say you are fat instead of carrying a child. That was done to trick the spirits and to protect the unborn child. For the first few weeks after a baby is born, it is called the 'little visitor', again to trick the spirits and to keep them away from the infant. The names given to a child are significant and are tied to their ancestors. Names are not to be discussed and decided beforehand like we do in America. To the Kipsigis, you are just asking for trouble when you do this.

All boys' names start with *Kip* and all girls' names start with *Chep*. This prefix is joined to a suffix which denotes something going on at the time of their birth or soon afterwards. For example, *lang'at* means night. A boy born at night would be called *Kiplang'at* and a girl would be called *Cheplang'at*. Some other examples are daytime—*bet*, afternoon—*rotich*, visitors—*toek*, or while you are outside—*sang'*, just to name a few. Our inside worker's name, Kipsang, means a boy that was born while the mother was outside. It was a bit unusual for a grown man to go by his childhood name, but for some reason, Kipsang preferred that over his 'adult' name of Joseph. Maybe because Joseph was such a common name and he wanted something different.

When we were in Kenya during our survey trip, Daryl learned to introduce himself as Daryl '*Arap*' *Bet*. *Arap* is the Kalenjin way to formally address a man. Introducing himself as *Arap Bet* always brought grins to their faces and we didn't know why until we learned that Bates sounded very similar to their word for daytime—*bet* (pronounced bait).They grinned because they were surprised a European, as we were called, could have the same name as an African. Saying my name brought its share of smiles, too. Laurie sounds similar to what they called a truck—a lorry (which phrase came from the British). When the two names were put together, it sounded like I was introducing myself as Day Truck.

However, I stopped introducing myself in that way when I found out that women and children don't bluntly introduce themselves by saying, 'I'm Laurie Bates' like a man would. Women and children took their identity from the family they were a part of or belonged to. At first I balked at saying I 'belonged' to Daryl as if I was his property. When I asked Antony why I had to say I belonged to someone, he explained that if women and children couldn't lay claim to a family, it meant you belonged to no one. You were all alone in the world. Who would want that? So, I soon learned to introduce myself by saying, *"Kainenyun ko Laurie nebo Dero Arap Bet*—My name is Laurie, the one belonging to Daryl Bates."

Everyone on our team received a Kipsigis name. Eddie Rogers, who is soft-spoken, was called *Arap Kalya*, the word for peace or quiet. Kevin Kehl, who kept a ruddy complexion from the Kenyan sun and has hairy arms, was called *Kipsabul Arap Birir*. This is the same phrase used in the Kalenjin Bible to describe Esau who was also known for being 'red and hairy'. Dave Vick, because of Vick's VapoRub was called *Arap Kerich,* the word for medicine. Given that *Arap Kerich* is the name usually reserved for witch doctors, he received bewildered looks whenever he, a white person, gave this as his Kipsigis name. Because Brenda came to Kenya with a baby, she was given the name, *Obotab* Josiah, mother of Josiah (her son's name).

All of this goes to show how much importance was given to a name. At the naming ceremony, as many members of the family that can come, do. The baby, referred to as, *tondet*—visitor, is placed in the middle of the gathering on a cowhide or in more modern times, a wool blanket. As the infant lay on the floor in their midst, the family members begin 'calling' ancestral names from the spirit world. Many peoples of the world have a cyclical worldview of life, death and re-incarnation, which goes on and on in an unending cycle. You don't always come back as yourself. It depends on how you've lived your life. This is quite opposite of the linear worldview held by the western culture, where you live and then you die. That's it. You only get one life to live.

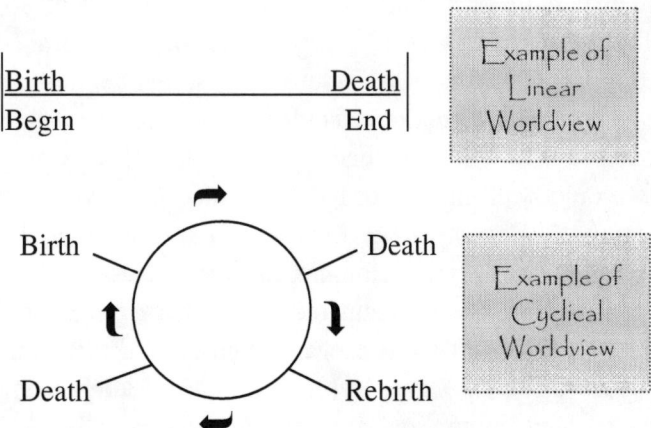

The infant lying on the floor, encircled by its' family, continues the cycle. After a name is called, the family audience waits to see if the child will acknowledge this ancestor by coughing or sneezing. If so, the ancestral spirit that has been 'called out' during the ceremony will 'inhabit' the child and the child will be 'called' that name from now on. (When I first heard the infant would cough or sneeze in acknowledgement of the ancestor, I thought the ceremony must take a long time. It wasn't until later when I had a newborn of my own that I realized how often that actually occurred.) Once the child in question coughed or sneezed, a designated member of the family (usually the oldest) spit a spray of home brew across the child's head. This was done as a show of acceptance on the family's part. If there was no brew available, they would spit whatever liquid was at hand. Many times milk was used as a substitute since it is so highly valued.

I couldn't believe that when I heard it. Spitting is such a sign of disdain in our culture. Even though spitting milk on an infant was more acceptable to me than spitting beer I just could not fathom why spitting, of all things, would be done. I had never heard of that before. But once something gets brought to your attention, you begin to notice it more. Throughout the years since then, I've noticed on TV or in movies, where people will use spitting as a way to ward off 'the evil eye'.

I found it humorous years later when watching the movie, <u>My Big Fat Greek Wedding</u>. As the bride walked down the aisle, her relatives made a show of spitting on her as she passed by. Her groom, standing at the front waiting for her to come to him, was watching aghast as this transpired. Reaching him, she saw his expression and paused to explain it was their way of warding off the 'evil eye' and in doing so, blessing her and their marriage. It was a funny scene in the movie, but I didn't find it so humorous when it happened to me.

Once the Kenyan ladies realized I was pregnant, they start asking me interesting questions. *Who was going to tightly wrap my stomach with a kanga after I gave birth to help flatten my stomach? Who was going to ceremonially shave the baby's head one month after the birth since my mother was in America?* When I told them we didn't do those types of things, they looked at me as strangely as I'm sure I was looking at them. Shaking their heads as in, 'you poor thing'; they told me to stay at home for six weeks after the birth to rest (holding up six fingers to emphasis their words).

Shortly after returning home from the birth of our daughter Lydia, Daryl resumed his work in the village. I was dutifully staying home, but I soon tired of it. Since we had run out of stamps and aerograms, I decided an outing to the Post Office would be the perfect first outing for us. Lydia was only about two weeks old and too small to fit safely in the front-load carrier I had. So instead, I used the Laleche League carrier I had been given by my teammate, Brenda Vick. This wide piece of cloth is folded in half lengthwise and worn sash-like from shoulder to hip. The construction of the carrier allows the infant to curl up in much the same manner and position as in the womb. It also evenly dispersed the weight across my back, making it comfortable for the both of us.

I determined that if the post office wasn't too taxing, I would pick up a few things at the market while I was out, too. Grabbing my market basket and shoving some shillings in my pocket, I set off. It felt wonderful to be out in the warm, brilliant sunshine. The lack of clouds made the sky seem incredibly blue and expansive. I was so glad I decided to go against convention and get out of the house. A leisurely fifteen-minute walk later, I was standing in the Sotik Post Office waiting my turn with the other people in the queue. When my turn arrived, I walked up to the chest high counter and told them what I wanted to purchase. Looking through their supplies to fill my request, they talked back and forth, glancing at me as they did so. I thought they were talking about stamps until I heard the word, *mtoto*—baby in Kiswahili and realized they were talking about me.

As we exchanged stamps and aerograms for money, one of the ladies asked in English, "Is that a baby?" motioning with her head to the bulge in my carrier.

(It was considered bad manners to point with your finger. Pointing with your finger was what you did when you counted livestock. To point to a person would be the same as lowering them to the level of a cow or a goat. So, instead of pointing like we do in the States, people motioned with their head or lip. Yes, by thrusting out their lower lip!)

"Yes." I proudly said. "She's two weeks old."

With a, "Tsk, tsk," she shook her head and said, "You should have stayed at home for another month!"

A bit deflated, I gathered my things to exit the building and walked down the sidewalk, leaving behind the fenced in compound of the Post Office. Just as I passed through this fence, another sidewalk began that took me further into town if

I chose to go that way. I paused at this juncture trying to make up my mind about what to do next.

Deciding to go ahead and do a bit of shopping, I turned away from the Post Office towards town. It was then that I noticed two little old ladies sitting side-by-side in the grass talking to each other and looking at me as they did so. Being in the minority here, I quickly learned that I made a scene wherever I went, without even trying. But a white baby seemed to be causing even more of a stir than usual. I nodded in casual greeting as I started past them, but one lady put up her hand in a halting motion and started speaking to me. I didn't understand what she was saying, but I did recognize that it was Kipsigis and not Kiswahili.

Using one of my much used phrases, I said, *"Tomagas Kipsigis komie*—I don't yet hear Kipsigis very well." She smiled and spoke to me again, this time more slowly. I still didn't catch everything she said, but I did hear the word, *lakwet*—baby in Kipsigis.

"Ee, lakwet—Yes, a baby!" I said, patting Lydia through the carrier.

Upon hearing this, she motioned with her head indicating she wanted to see inside. New mothers love to show off their babies and I was no different. Smiling with pride, I bent over and opened up the carrier so they could see her. The ladies looked inside, nodding, smiling and talking amongst them-selves again. (*Probably saying she's the most beautiful baby they'd ever seen!!*) That thought made me grin and I moved a bit closer to give them a better view.

Then the next thing I knew one of the ladies spit, with perfect accuracy, between the edges of the fabric I was holding open, onto the cheek of my little sleeping angel. A myriad of thoughts raced through my mind at that moment...*indignation, shock and the rampant tuberculosis in the area.* But before I could act on any of those feelings, a thought came bouncing to the forefront of my brain from the cultural studies we had done. *Spitting is not a show of disgust. It is meant as a blessing.* I'm sure my eyes were bugging out of my head, but I finally managed to pull myself together enough to gasp out a *"Kongoi*—thank you."

After doing so, I shut the edges of the carrier together; made an about face and headed for home. As I got to a bend in the road, I looked back to see if the ladies were still visible. They were not. Opening the fabric, I reached inside, removed the spittle from her cheek and wiped it onto my skirt.

After that I pulled her out, clutched her to me and said, "I'm so sorry, Sweetie. Mommy's so sorry!"

Lydia had slept through the whole incident, none the wiser, but my rough handling woke her up and made her cry. When she started crying, I did too. Gently, I patted and rubbed her back, calming down the both of us. Lydia once again fell asleep. I resumed the trip back home with Lydia in my arms.

After a few minutes, I chuckled to myself and said, "Well, I guess I should have listened to everyone and just stayed home!"

Lesson Learned

Blessings can come from people and places you <u>never</u> could have imagined. Don't disregard them simply because they are not in the package you expect.

This was actually a Ladies Meeting I attended with teammate, Susan Kehl. But the setting is so similar to the 'Spit A Blessing' incident with my daughter, Lydia, that I thought to include it here. (You can easily imagine my hands holding open the fabric of the carrier)

EIGHT
sisit

(see seat)

*"If you think you are wise by the world's
standards, you will have to become a fool so
you can become wise by God's standards. For
the wisdom of this world is foolishness to God."*
I Corinthians 3:18 (NLT)

TEA AND A
PURPLE SWEATER

Unlikely as it may seem, there are options available to every
woman who gives birth to a baby in Kenya. However, because
of cost, convenience, culture and modesty, most of the local
women gave birth in their huts. They would shoo the men away
(who were more than happy to absent themselves from the
proceedings) and called the village ladies in to assist with the
childbirth. Only when something seemed to be going wrong,
did they use outside help. Some of the missionary ladies who
had lived in Kenya for a while, opted to have their babies at
home just like the Kenyan ladies. Other missionary ladies used

the local clinics. But after hearing that cats and chickens were allowed to freely walk around inside, I chose not to use them to have our baby. We did use the local clinics and hospitals for minor things, but I didn't want to use them for a possible surgery. All of my sisters had to have caesarean childbirths. My mother had all six of her children naturally. Since I wasn't sure what type of childbirth I would have, I wanted something a bit more modern than what the rural health facilities had to offer.

The best hospitals were in or near Nairobi. These were the most modern hospitals, not only in Kenya, but in East Africa. Doctors from all over Africa and Europe worked in them and they all spoke some English. But the accents were sometimes so heavy it was hard (for me, at least) to understand what they were saying. It wasn't only the accents that sometimes made using these doctors difficult. It was also the different medical terms, medicines prescribed and general terminology used that differed from country to country. Not wanting to expend the energy figuring out what they were saying in the throes of labor, I opted to use an America mission hospital just outside of Nairobi in the Great Rift Valley called Kijabe Medical Centre. Kijabe wasn't quite as modern as Nairobi Hospital, but the doctors and many of head nurses were American and I had no problem understanding them.

Nairobi is a four to six hour drive from Sotik depending on the weather and the condition of the roads. Because of this distance, missionary families often traveled into Nairobi ten to fourteen days before the due date (just in case the baby came early), so they could be near a modern hospital. Staying in hotels for an extended time like that was costly. Whenever we went into Nairobi, we usually stayed two to three days if our schedule allowed, to stock up on supplies, to eat out in a restaurant or to go to the movies. (We did this about three to four times a year.) To help out missionaries and their visitors, different church groups built 'guest houses' for them to stay in which charged a more reasonable rate. This definitely helped, not only because it was more economical, but because they were more family-friendly. You could meet other missionary families from all over East Africa there. It was always nice to meet fellow Americans, catch up on news from the States and to hear about their work. There were times the guest houses were full and we would ask a Nairobi missionary family if we could stay with them.

One of the people we all stayed with at one time or another was a single missionary lady named, Carla Dean Thompson or CDT, as she likes to be called. She always had a room ready for us to stay in. Carla Dean only asked the people that stayed with her to pay for their food and to give her worker a little something for the extra work that we caused him. She saw keeping people in her home as a ministry, which it definitely was! Carla Dean was often the first one to see our new additions and she genuinely oohed and aahed in the stead of our families. She lovingly became known to all the kids as Aunt Carla Dean. Her home was a great place for expectant families to hang out while they waited to go into labor and then to recuperate afterwards. We all knew that as soon as we got back home, we wouldn't have much help with the new baby, so we took advantage of the pampering she always gave us.

Not long after that first surprising outing at the post office, Antony Marusoi, our language helper, asked if we would be home the next day at 2 p.m. (He often set up meetings at new places for us to try to start new churches or just to have an informal visit with Kipsigis. These meetings improved our language skills and helped us to get to know the other areas where our Kipsigis Christian brothers and sisters lived.)

Thinking Antony had a special outing in mind, Daryl told him, "Yes, the car is available if you want to go somewhere."

"No." Antony said. "We want to give you a *chaikab lakwet*—a tea for the baby." Or, as we would say, a baby shower.

Bill from Lydia's birth (the 1432/= is about $85)

Having attended several of these by now, I was both pleased and overwhelmed at the same time. I was pleased, because it was the community's way of showing we were being accepted among them (like the old ladies spitting on us outside the post office). But, I was overwhelmed because I knew all the work that was involved in having one of these types of meetings. In American baby showers, all the refreshments are provided for the new mother and all she has to do is show up. For the Kenyan baby 'tea', I was the one who prepared everything for our guests. So much for sitting back and pampering myself!!

Not knowing who all would be attending this event, I asked Antony what was the proper protocol to follow. Antony told us he would be the one to coordinate things. Relieved to hear this, we discussed what food we should serve and how many people he thought we should plan for. After all of this was decided, we asked him to explain everything to Kipsang so we could all work together on it. For formal gatherings, a meal was expected. But thankfully, Antony said simple bread and butter sandwiches with chaik were all that would be required. I was also relieved that everything for this simple meal could be purchased here in town, so gathering all we needed for the meal, at such short notice, wouldn't be difficult.

Our bread came unsliced in a printed wax paper wrapper, with words that boasted it had 'extra fat and sugar' as its selling point. Coming from a sugar-free, fat-free America, that came as a surprise when we first arrived in Kenya. Since we had been there over a year, we hardly even noticed it. What we did pay attention to was the scarcity of the wax paper the bread wrapper was made of. Wax paper was one of the items we put on our 'Nairobi shopping list'. Those items were things we could not find locally, so we looked for them whenever we went into the 'big city'. Because of its scarcity in our little town of Sotik, the wrapper was carefully removed, crumbs brushed off, paper neatly folded and stored for future use. The bread, now free of its prized wrappings, was cut into one inch thick slices ready to have the 'butter' spread on it.

The 'butter' part of the sandwiches was not real butter at all. Real butter was available, but because of the scarcity of electricity, most people used a tinned margarine called Blue Band. This bright yellow can had a large band of blue wrapping around it. 'Blue Band' could be found in very remote places. It ranged in size from a small can that held about one cup to the size I kept on hand which weighed one kilo or 2.2 pounds. Once the can was opened, there were no lids to keep it closed. So we kept it covered with plastic wrap or foil and a rubber band to hold the cover in place. After coming for a visit, Louise Cole, an elder's wife from our overseeing congregation, determined she would find lids for us when she returned to America. She traced a circle around a can of Blue Band to take home as a template. Soon afterwards, I started receiving them in the mail. They fit! Louise said it was the plastic lid that came from a medium-sized can of coffee. When she put out word at church to save them for us, I soon had so many, that I started giving them away. The recipients, both Kenyan and American, were thrilled to get them.

Chaik in Kenya is made up of three simple ingredients— tea leaves, milk and sugar. City folk and East Indians liked to add a touch of masala spice which makes it taste more like the Chai Tea Latte you get at coffee shops here in America. The most used brand of tea was KETEPA, which is short for Kenya Tea Packers. There are tea estates, both with vast acreage and tiny home plots, all over Kenya including Kericho District, the area we lived in. Just like Blue Band, KETEPA could be found in remote places. The most common size sold was a tiny package that is about 1"x 1½"x 3" and had loose leaves. I bought the bagged kind for myself because it was easier to clean up and dispose of after brewing. Daryl and our workers preferred the loose leaves. So I usually bought a big bag of tea leaves about the size of a bag of coffee and boxes of fifty-count bagged tea.

In our area of the country, there was only one brand of milk for purchase and that came from the Kenya Creamery Company, or KCC. One of their creameries was across the valley from our houses. In the vast darkness that surrounded us at night because of the lack of street lights, it was comforting to look across the way to see the lights twinkling over at the factory. KCC milk came in the refrigerated form like we have in the US. But instead of the carton or plastic jug we were used to, it came in a two-cup packet shaped like a triangle. There was also a shelf milk that had been Ultra Heat Treated. It was called UHT for short and came in a small rectangular box which held around two cups like the other milk. It was called 'shelf' milk because it required no refrigeration and could just sit out on your shelf until it was opened. I purchased this by the case and kept it on hand for cooking and chaik making, reserving the fresh milk (because it tasted better) for drinking and eating cereal. The UHT milk was also good to have on hand to give out to people who came to the door looking for a hand-out or as something to give as a 'hostess gift' to the villagers when we went for a visit.

Kipsang, Daryl and I went into the kitchen to try to figure out what supplies we needed based upon what we had on hand and the number of people Antony said he thought would come. With the loaves of bread being about eight inches long and the bread being cut in one inch slices, we would only get about four sandwiches for each loaf of bread. We used this as an estimate for how many loaves would be required and sent Daryl into town to pick up more bread along with a case of UHT milk, sugar, tea and Blue Band.

Kipsang estimated that we needed to make five gallons of chaik, which was the size of the *sufaria*—cooking pot I used to boil water everyday. So he boiled the next day's water in advance and got the kitchen in readiness. I looked around the house for chairs and moved furniture around to accommodate the extra pieces. (When we packed the container to come to Kenya, I threw in an old card table and four folding chars when I realized there was room for them. I can't tell you how many times we used those! For the first few months they served as our dining room table and chairs until we found a set we wanted to purchase. I don't think I regretted a single item we packed and shipped over in that container.)

Upon Daryl's return from town, Kipsang and I began slicing the bread for the sandwiches. I never appreciated the saying, 'the greatest thing since sliced bread' before that day. When we got a good amount of bread cut, I started applying the Blue Band. Smearing on what I thought was a generous amount, Kipsang shook his head and showed me the 'proper' amount to put on—a ¼ to ½ inch thickness! After cutting the sandwiches in half diagonally, they were ready to be served. We started piling them on sufaria lids and covering them with plastic wrap to keep them fresh for tomorrow. (Because *sufaria* lids are large, round and flat, I kept several on hand to use as platters, pizza pans and cookie sheets.)

After lunch the next day, Kipsang started preparing the chaik. I got out all the mugs and coffee cups we had. Daryl and I checked the living room and kitchen one more time to make sure everything was ready. With nothing more we could think of to do, we just sat back and waited for our visitors to arrive. Around two p.m., people started showing up, arriving on foot. Some had walked for miles in order to come. Because the things in my house were so different from theirs, I'm sure they had to restrain themselves from staring and touching things as they came into the house, in much the same way I did when I first entered their huts. As each person entered, we shook hands and exchanged greetings. After a while, Antony stood to begin the ceremony. He thanked everyone for coming, led them in a few songs, followed by a sermonette. (Every gathering was used to teach others about God.)

I realized he was winding down when I heard Jehovah and *lakwet*—baby used together a couple of times. I didn't make out all he said, since it was in Kipsigis, but I inferred from the bits I did understand that he was asking God to bless our baby. This was confirmed when he looked at me and asked me to bring in the baby. I had left Lydia asleep in our bedroom.

Sotik living room, Lydia is not quite one year old

She fussed a bit as I picked her up and woke her from her sound sleep. Re-entering the living room, Antony directed me to a different chair that had been repositioned so that it faced everyone. After I sat down, he told me they would now begin praying over the child. Cradled in my arms, our daughter Lydia settled back to sleep as a prayer was offered up for her in a language neither she nor I yet fully understood.

Antony concluded the prayer, said a few more words and then the group began singing again. While this song was being sung, people began to shuffle about with their belongings, bringing out items I had not noticed before. I knew from experience that gifts were given at *chaikab lakwets*, but because we were considered wealthy, I figured they wouldn't bring us gifts. I was mistaken. One by one, they stood up and laid their gifts for Lydia on our coffee table...fresh brown eggs, a paper sack of stone-ground corn, bundles of *sukuma wiki* (leafy greens similar to spinach or kale), bright red tomatoes, purple onions and dried beans—all the items that made up a typical day's meal and probably came from their own gardens. It wasn't until someone pulled out a recycled glass bottle filled with milk, with a corncob used as a stopper, that I realized the sacrifice that had been made on our behalf that day.

I must have hugged Lydia tightly to me in my anxiety because she cried out. Using this as an excuse to leave, I went to find Daryl who had left after receiving everyone into our home. (He absented himself from the activities for the same reason that men don't usually go to baby showers in the US.) Shutting the door behind me as I entered our bedroom, I walked up to Daryl.

Tearfully I told him, "Daryl, they are giving too much! I know some of them are giving us the food they were going to eat today! *We don't need it. They need it.* How can I get them to take it back?"

Putting his hand on my arm to calm me down, he said, "Laurie, you can't do that. Don't you realize they are trying to bless us and Lydia? If you try to give their gifts back it's like you're refusing them and what they are trying to do for us. You would be robbing them of the blessing they receive, too, when they give to others."

Seeing the wisdom in his words, I dried my eyes, took a deep breath to calm myself down and returned to the living room where the singing had continued in my absence. After I returned, more produce, milk, eggs and flour were put on the table. Someone even laid down a brilliant purple hand-knitted sweater. Crying is a faux pas, so I was struggling mightily to keep from doing so. But when Antony laid down a fifty shilling note, a day's wages, I couldn't control the tear that slipped down my cheek. Unobtrusively, I wiped it away. Soon afterwards, the singing stopped.

Antony stood, turned to me and said, "Now it is time for you to say something."

Reciting the words I learned to say at every gathering, "*Kainenyun ko Laurie, nebo Dero Arap Bet*—My name is Laurie, the one belonging to Mr. Daryl Bates. "*Abaibai mising agatak en kainetab Jesu*—I'm very happy to greet you in the name of Jesus."

Then I started thanking them for the gifts they had brought.. "*Kongoi*— thank you *agobo*—for the *maainik*—eggs, *sukuma wiki*—greens, *bandek*—corn, *chego*—milk *ak ng'wek*—and vegetables. *Kongoi agobo age tugul*—thank you for everything!"

Kenyan stamp showing women working in a field

I'm not sure what else I said. I know I switched over to English at some point to thank them for coming and for the other gifts that were given that I couldn't remember the words for. I also know it was not with the depth of emotion I was feeling at that moment. It must have been satisfactory though because there were heads nodding and smiles all around as I resumed my seat. Soon after I finished speaking, Antony ended with a prayer for the food and Kipsang walked in with a platter of sandwiches.

Relieved to have something I knew how to do, I practically flew into the kitchen gathering up mugs and the pot of chaik. Daryl must have been listening out of view because he came into the kitchen to take Lydia so I could serve our guests. Giving me a smile of encouragement, he went into the living room to eat, to visit with the guests and to also thank them for their gifts, which unlike me, he did with ease.

Several cups of chaik and many sandwiches later, our guests asked for permission to leave, as was the custom, so they could reach home before it got dark. We granted them the permission they asked for, so they started gathering their things. Shaking our hands as they filed out past us, they began their long walk home. I was again humbled by the way they so sacrificially gave to us and thought nothing of the long walk to our home and then back again.

Quickly, Daryl and I got the house back in order as Kipsang finished washing the dishes. He had such a large family that he was always happy to bring home anything extra, so I had him bundle up the leftover bread and butter sandwiches. When he was finished with that, I told him to go on home, too, before it got dark. Daryl and I put away the milk, produce, eggs and flour and felt blessed all over again by their giving. He took the money into our bedroom as I looked more closely at the purple sweater.

Not knowing how to knit, I wondered how much time it must have taken to make it and I imagined on what she was doing as she knitted…listened to the radio, waited for water to boil, watched livestock or visited with a neighbor. Lydia only wore the sweater once and that was when we went to visit the person who had knitted it. Since she was born during Kenya's 'summer' I felt it was never cool enough to warrant such a heavy sweater. Even though Kenyan Mamas had the practice of wrapping their babies up until they broke out with little beads of sweat.

I think it is interesting to note that as a teenager, my daughter learned to knit and loves creating gifts for people. And, that as much as I dressed my 'peaches and cream' complexioned little girl in pinks and pastels, one of her favorite colors (to this day) is purple. I wish I had kept that little handmade sweater as a keepsake for her. But instead, I gave it away at a *chaikab lakwet* for another child. I knew the recipient would actually wear it and get a lot more use out of it than I ever would.

That day was a turning point in my life and missionary career. Going to East Africa to teach, I never thought about the things I myself would be taught. That experience helped me to realize that at heart we all care about the same things: family and home.

LESSON LEARNED

*Don't refuse to allow people to sacrificially give.
There is a grace in giving but there is also a grace
in receiving. We need to learn how to do both.*

Lydia and I sharing a meal with some of
the ladies after a meeting. This meal
truly is a 'dinner on the grounds'

nine

sOgOl
(so goal)

"When destiny calls you, you must be strong."
Song: <u>You'll Be in My Heart</u> by Phil Collins

THE DAILY
(UN)ROUTINE

In America we are driven by the 9 to 5 work cycle which tends to make a pattern or rhythm for us to fall into. In Kenya, we had no such schedule because there were so many daily unforeseen events that occurred to disturb our best laid plans. Interruptions to our day so often occurred, that we began using an expression we had heard others say when we first arrived, because it so aptly described so many situations. That expression was and still is, 'T.I.A.—This Is Africa!' Since these unexpected occurrences were so frequent, we would also say, "The only thing you can depend on is that nothing will go the way you planned." But after saying all this, I'll try to reconstruct my day-to-day activities for you as best as I can (when things *did* work out as I planned, that is).

Typically, Sunday was our long day out in the village for 'church'. Mondays, we tried to take a day off and do activities away from home to get rejuvenated. Tuesday was our team meeting day. Wednesdays through Saturdays were used as additional office days and/or days to go out into the village. I'll skip Sunday and Monday for now and begin with Tuesday.

On Tuesday mornings, the men met to discuss things pertaining to 'work'. We rotated these meetings between our houses. Whoever hosted the meeting provided something for the guys to eat at 'chaik time' other than the usual bread and butter sandwiches our workers ate. We made things like banana or zucchini bread, breakfast casserole, or cinnamon rolls— whatever it was, we made it from scratch. When the meetings were over, the men adjourned to their own homes. There they worked on lessons for the upcoming week, correspondence or newsletters for the rest of the day. After supper, the entire team would get together to discuss upcoming events or points of interest that affected the whole team.

One example would be when Brenda suggested a cement pad be made so their son, Josiah (and later on our kids when they got big enough), could have a place to ride a tricycle, draw with chalk and other things like that, that couldn't be done on grass. As a team, (with the guys input) we decided to put in a half-sized cement basketball court. That way, kids and adults alike could get use out of it. We split the cost of building the court between us. When we decided to enclose our yards for privacy, we discussed the type of tree to use for the hedge and then whom to hire to deliver and plant all those trees; again dividing the cost between us. Another time, after the Vicks house got broken into while we were all away in Nairobi, we decided to hire an *askari*—night watchman, to patrol the compound at night and on days that we were not there. We also discussed monthly meetings, upcoming trips to Nairobi or other cities, in case someone wanted us to purchase food stuffs or other items while we were there. After our business was concluded, we had dessert, then play some type of game or just visited and let the kids play together once they started coming along. Usually whoever hosted the men that morning hosted that meeting too. It just made it easier to keep track of who was doing what, when.

Building basketball court with summer interns' help

On Wednesday mornings, the ladies met. Many of the discussions that had occurred the day before would be planned further by us. Our meetings seemed to revolve around food. We discussed the feeding of the *askari*—night watchman, the feeding of the people planting the trees for our hedge or what food items we would like to be picked up for us. We also discussed upcoming monthly meetings to know who was coming, who would need a place to stay, whose house it would be at and what items we needed to borrow from each other for this event. The men came up with the ideas and we ladies worked out a lot of the details.

With so much of our focus being on food and all of those recipes having to be made from scratch, food prep took up a lot of our time. We bought food in bulk where we could, then subdivided and froze it. After buying one too many (expensive) frozen chickens with freezer-burn, Brenda came up with the idea of buying live chickens and having our workers kill and clean them. She or Dave would drive into the compound with about fifteen to twenty live chickens in the back of their covered truck. Our inside workers would gather around, picking them up by their feet and carry them off to the back of the yard by our large compost pit.

There was no trash pick-up in our town. We each kept a small compost bucket that we put eggshells, coffee grounds, tea leaves, vegetable peelings and other organic matter into. And, each family had their own little garden plots and composts pits where the organic matter was allowed to decompose with other things from the yard and garden and later used as fertilizer. We all shared one very large garbage pit where our trash was burned. It was a common occurrence to see kids scampering out of it with tin cans and other non-burnable objects that they remade into toys and other items.

Beside that large communal compost pit was where they would each carry out a large pot of hot water to help in the chicken butchering and dressing process. I don't know what all they did to dress them; I didn't really want to know. I was just thankful for the nice-looking platter of cut-up, skinned chicken that would be waiting on the counter for me to cook, debone, chop and freeze. If it had been left up to me to slaughter the meat we ate, we would have become vegetarians. Growing up in a sterile grocery store age, it would have been hard for me to look a live animal in the eye and then make a finished, dressed product out of it. Kipsang seemed to enjoy this day because it got him outside of the house and away from doing *his* daily routine of housework for a large part of the day and a chance to hang out with the 'other guys.' Another perk for Kipsang was that he got the lion's share of the chicken. All I wanted from the chickens were the breasts, the thighs and the legs, and those skinned. So Kipsang got to take the rest of the chicken home to his family for his wife to make a rich soup with all the organ parts of the chicken that the Kipsigis thought of as a delicacy. That seemed only fitting since he did all the work of preparing the chicken. (Since he prepared so many chickens at one time and had no electricity at his house, he would sometimes divide this into smaller bundles and then store them in my freezer.)

Since my stomach was, and still is, very squeamish at the sight of blood, imagine my surprise when my three-year old, Lydia, wanted to go out and watch the chickens being butchered. I tried to tactfully explain what was going to happen. When that didn't dissuade her, I became more graphic. She still wanted to go. So, I let her, thinking she would come running back in tears, but she didn't. To this day, she still likes to watch what I consider gruesome surgeries and procedures; while I sit there with my eyes covered waiting for her to tell me when it's over. Because of my sensitive stomach and nose, meat seemed to be the worst thing for me to buy.

In large towns, you could pick up refrigerated meat at the 'butchery'. In our town, there was little, if any, refrigeration and that not very reliable. The cows and goats which were slaughtered a short distance away, were brought into town on a donkey or cow drawn wooden cart. Outside the door of the butchery shop, there were wooden crates upon which the heads of the slaughtered animals were placed to show what kinds of meats were available for purchase. Their dressed carcasses hung behind the store front glass display window.

Going inside, you would tell the man how many kilos (2.2 pounds) of 'fillet' you wanted to purchase. He then opened the screened door, hacked off a portion from the carcass and then put this onto a bloody hanging scale. (Similar to the type you see in American grocery stores to weigh produce.) If the amount of meat was more than you asked for, he took the meat out of the scale and plopped it onto a blood soaked stump (used as a chopping block) and cut off a bit, then reweighed it. The whole process was rather crude. I usually took whatever amount he hacked off so the meat came in contact with as little of these blood soaked items as possible.

After our survey trip, I asked my dad to show me the meat chart of a cow and a diagram of how to cut up a chicken so I could be better prepared when we moved to Kenya. (He used to teach agriculture so he knows about all this stuff and had the charts.) After showing me the diagrams, he had me cut up a chicken. When I finished, I told him it was gross and I didn't see know how Mom could do it all the time. Because of my reaction then, I surprised him a few years later when they came to visit us in Kenya.

During their visit I would tell them whenever I was going into town to run an errand, in case they wanted to 'tag along' to see our day-to-day activities or to take pictures or to just look around at the workings of an African town. On that occasion, I told my dad, "If you'd like to come, I'm going into town to buy some meat. I want to get to the butchery shop before the flies get too bad."

He got quite a chuckle out of me saying that because it was so different from how I would have reacted before going to Kenya. He still reminds me about it from time to time. Over the years, the 'butchery' didn't bother me like it did at first. When I was newly pregnant, the smell of blood and the sight of flies everywhere, about made me gag on the spot. I literally couldn't stomach going into the 'butchery' to purchase the meat, so we did without beef for a while until Daryl noticed and asked why. After explaining how I felt, he simply said, "Just send Kipsang into town and have him do it."

That simple statement opened up my mind to not only that task, but to all sorts of possibilities. Yes, Kipsang was there to help me with housework, but he could help me with other things, too. When you are not used to having someone work in your home, it takes some time to get adjusted to the idea. With this new concept in mind, I tried to think of conveniences I didn't have and to see if there was a way Kipsang could either make or 'be' those conveniences for me.

Since having something home delivered wasn't an option, I sent Kipsang to town to pick up small things when Daryl was out with the car. I taught Kipsang how to use the food processor, so he could grind the meat instead of me. Without fast food chains available, I taught him how to make soups and stew, so supper could be waiting for us when we came home after being away all day. I had him make pie crusts to put into the freezer, slice and grate cheese which we bought in big blocks, chop vegetables to be placed in the refrigerator or freezer, cook and debone chicken. Anything I could think to have him do (ahead of time) to make cooking easier for me, I started having him do those things.

Since he was struggling with English, and I was struggling with Kalenjin, I drew a picture recipe book that showed what I wanted him to make. I broke down the recipe bit by bit, holding up each measuring implement he would use to make it and asked him to say the words slowly in Kalenjin so I could write them down. Since I wasn't sure what his reading level was, I drew pictures as well as writing down the instructtions so he would know how to prepare the recipe when he was there by himself.

For the first nine months, we didn't have electricity, so all of our clothes were washed by hand. After the electricity came, we used our washing machine. (It was fun to see Kipsang watching the clothes being washed by the machine.) Either way, there always seemed to be clothes or diapers that needed washing. After the clothes were washed, either by Kipsang or me, they were hung out on a clothes line to dry. Since Kipsang (and Joseph) were only there for part of the day, there was usually something still wet that had to be brought in later after it dried.

One day, Kathy surprised me when she said she noticed Kipsang hanging out our diapers on the clothes line. She wanted to know how I got him to this because her worker wouldn't touch theirs. I told her it had never been an issue between us. Kipsang just did anything we asked of him; both he and Joseph were that way. Since we had never had anyone work in our home before, I just assumed everyone's workers acted the same way ours did. I had not realized until then how blessed we were to have such excellent helpers.

So, if most mornings were filled with household chores, cleaning and food prep, most of the afternoons from Wednesday to Saturday were spent 'out' in the village. Normally we went to the same places, but wherever Antony worked out for us to go, we went. We would leave around 2 p.m., drive thirty to forty-five minutes, bouncing along on dirt roads/paths most of the way. Arriving at the homestead, we walked a short distance to the host's hut where we were served chaik while we waited for everyone to arrive. We would then have a Bible study or service for a few hours; conclude with more chaik and visiting and then leave. Because there were no street lights, the roadways really got dark out in the villages at sunset. With so many people walking about, we tried to leave just before dusk so it wouldn't be pitch black as we drove though the twisting and turning country lanes. Arriving home we had a simple meal; grilled cheese and soup, leftovers from lunch, or breakfast foods because I didn't feel like making a big meal after being out in the village for the bulk of the day.

After I started having babies, I didn't go out as much with Daryl, so I made a nice meal prepared for us to share when he got home. When I did go with kids in tow, I went to the places nearby. Just Daryl and Antony would go when they went to new places or towns far away. Meetings of any sort tended to be segregated affairs; men on one side, women and children on the other. Since I was basically on my own to take care of the kids, I waited until the kids were more manageable before going far away or to places I didn't know well.

Having kids definitely changed my perspective on things. Everything I did was scrutinized by the African 'mamas'! And all the things I brought to keep my children busy were scrutinized by the Kenyan kids. One time, I gave Lydia a little swat on the leg to discipline her during a church service. Noticing this, an old woman 'tsk, tsked' me and told me, "*Achicha, boisetab lagok*—No, that is the work of children."

At a meeting when Daryl's parents come for a visit

Saturday morning was another time we ladies tried to claim for ourselves. After we all had more than one child, we decided to create our own 'Mom's Day Out' program. I don't know whose idea it was initially. But, we each brought different thoughts of what we would like to see accomplished during that time and wound up making a good program for the kids and ourselves. I, for one, was proud of our little Mom's Day Out program. It was nice to feel like I was making a helpful contribution to the team. Plus, I enjoyed the creative outlet this program gave me. Our line up included a Bible class, a snack, a 'hands on' activity or a game and then lunch.Because sitting still in an American 'Sunday School' had been difficult for some of the kids, we decided to put that in the program. Part of this time was used to teach our kids the little American songs we had been taught as kids. That way, the next time the kids went on furlough and sat in American Bible classes; the American songs would be more familiar to them. It also taught them from an early age that there were times you needed to sit still, listen and learn.

When we first started up this program, it was in-between our furloughs, so we used a hodgepodge of leftover Sunday school material I had brought back the last time we were in the US. Our overseeing congregation was in Muskogee, OK, where there is a large Cherokee population. Bacone College, an American Indian university, was having a 'garage sale' and I picked up material from there. All organizations that use teaching materials have bits and pieces leftover that they don't know what to do with and hate to throw away. The Muskogee church had these and they told me I could take what I wanted. But the reason I chose the material from the American Indian college was that there was not a blond-haired, blue-eyed illustration in the bunch! All the illustrations had dark vivid coloring which was more appropriate to the African culture and skin tones. I originally bought these with the thought of trying to teach a Kenyan Sunday School when we went out in the villages, but as of yet had not taken the opportunity to use them. (I became pregnant shortly after returning from furlough and was nauseous for most of the pregnancy.)

Brenda, who had the only child old enough to be home-schooled, said it would be helpful to her if we could work art into the program. So we put the 'hands-on' activity in our Mom's Day Out to help her. I enjoyed the challenge of trying to figure out art projects or hands-on activities to go with the lessons. When we were doing the lesson on Jonah and the Big Fish, we made up a fish piñata for our activity. We bashed it open the next week at Lydia's Little Mermaid® themed birth-day party. A hands-on activity we did, when we were learning about creation, was a 'create-your-own pizza face' using ham, cheese and vegetables cutouts. These were baked and then later eaten for lunch. That was such a hit, that I tried to tie in food whenever I could. Another food item the kids really enjoyed was butterfly/ angel sandwiches. After making up the sandwich of your choice, you turned them on the diagonal; cut out the center strip and then inverted the sides. The kids started asking for angel or butterfly sandwiches a lot after that. It was funny how some-thing that simple could get a child to eat a sandwich when they didn't want to eat it before.

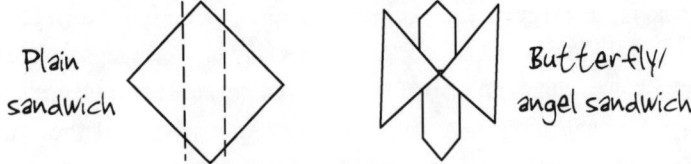

Plain sandwich   Butterfly/ angel sandwich

There wasn't anything specific I wanted accomplished with my kids for the Mom's Day Out. I just wanted a break and as long of a time as we could stretch it out to! As much as I love my children, sometimes you just have to take some time for yourself to recharge your batteries. We initially had our program run from 8:30 a.m. to 11 a.m., which didn't really give me the time I was looking for. But when we added on a lunch to the program, it made it last longer and ran from around 9 a.m. to 1 p.m. Now, whenever it was my turn to be 'off' of the Mom's Day Out rotation, Daryl and I would hop in the car and drive to Kericho, a town about thirty minutes away, so we could try to squeeze in a date or run errands we needed to do together that were difficult to get done with small children.

An additional thing we ladies did on Saturdays, or on another day of the week, was to have Ladies' Meetings out in the village, on our own. We started at first with the ladies from the first Sotik team, Cyndi Chowning and Janet Allison. Then after a bit, we eventually started going out by ourselves like the guys did. I started by going out about twice a month. The week before I would go out, I prepared a simple lesson and had Antony break it down phonetically for me in Kipsigis. But, I got so tense and nervous that I was short tempered and irritable all week. The whole experience was so stressful to me that I cut back to once a month instead of twice, hoping this would help lessen the tension. It didn't.

When Daryl asked why I was having such a bad attitude, I explained that my Kipsigis language skills were so bad, that I didn't know what I was saying half the time when I presented my lessons. And, that I could barely understand what was being asked of me when I was out in the village. It made me feel stupid. I couldn't understand why it was so difficult for me to learn a language. Most things in life that I had tried to do, I was able to find a way to do them. But, for some reason, language was something I simply could not seem to get a handle on and it was both aggravating and humiliating!

Finally getting it off my chest, I said, "The one thing I enjoy is being able to pick up the ladies in the truck and take them to different areas they normally don't get to go to. When I do this, it gives them the opportunity to visit with women they wouldn't get to see otherwise. It is such a treat for them. The women get so few treats here, that I am happy to be able to do this one simple thing for them. But it is the only thing I enjoy about the whole experience!"

He told me, "You know, you can't hide your feelings. They show clearly on your face. You're not fooling anybody, especially not the Kenyans. I think you should just stay home until you can go back out again with a good attitude."

My response was, "But the other ladies on our team are going out. How can I just stay home? Isn't that one of the reasons we came, so that I could teach, too?"

Daryl said, "Yes, that's true. But just because you choose not to go out to teach the ladies does *not* mean you're not helping *us* to do missions. Managing our home, taking care of our family, preparing meals, receiving visitors and all the other things you do, take a load off of me. You have created a haven for me to come home to after being out in the village all day. When you do all those things, and you do them well," he added with a smile, "you allow me to focus on the things I need to. So don't *ever* think you're not doing your part just because you don't go out to teach the ladies. Anyway, whether you realize it or not, you <u>are</u> teaching them how to be a Christian wife and mother whenever we go anywhere because they are watching everything you do."

This conversation carried on in much the same manner until I realized Daryl truly meant what he said and wasn't just saying these things to make me feel better. A huge weight was lifted off of my shoulders that day. I took a moment to mentally list all the things I did for us and our children. Then I looked at them again from the perspective of Daryl having to do all of it along with the teaching he did, too. Now, instead of feeling like I was not 'doing my part', it gave purpose to the things I was doing and helped me to understand that even though I hadn't realized it, I was doing a lot to keep us on the field.

Being among the Kipsigis people, Wednesday through
Sunday, we tried to take a break on Mondays and Tuesdays and
use those days for ourselves. Sometimes we simply stayed at
home with the curtains drawn, but that didn't deter people from
stopping by. All hours of the day or night, we were expected to
make something to eat for our Christian brothers or sisters who
stopped by or, if it was dark, a place for them to sleep. Because
we always felt like we were 'on-call', we never considered
ourselves as 'off duty' until we were in Nairobi or some other
place away from the Kipsigis people we served. Yes, I admit
this got tedious at times; even annoying when you were in the
middle of something that you had to stop and set aside until
later. Especially if I was about to put in a video for the kids to
watch or work on a large project that required the large area the
living room provided. If we were eating a meal that we knew
the Kipsigis wouldn't eat like spaghetti (they thought it looked
like bloody worms), we would have to put that meal aside and
make up something they would eat. But, I learned to keep
loaves of bread in the freezer and the pantry stocked with sodas
and the makings for chaik. With these things on hand, it was
easier to feed unexpected visitors something simple whenever
they happened to show up.

In order to better and more easily accommodate our
guests, Daryl asked our landlord if we could add on to our
house. We were still renting the Chowning house to use as
office space and as a sleeping area for guests. But after the
Kehls moved away, it didn't feel as secure as it once did. Our
team was also beginning to have summer interns and guests
from America that needed their own space for the weeks that
they stayed with us. When the landlord agreed, we told our
team during one of our weekly meetings. Everyone decided to
add on to their homes, too. As a result, we quit renting the
Chowning's house down the lane.

With no architect handy, I drew up simple plans for the
builders to use. Each plan was as unique as the person who

designed it. We each added on an office, a guestroom and a space to entertain guests *outside* of our houses. Brenda and I also included a laundry/storage space and an outside guest bathroom into our plans. With the washing machine needing to be filled by bucket a lot of the time, water tended to splash making a mess in the pantry where our washing machines were set up. By moving them out of this space, we didn't have to worry so much about making a mess. Brenda's entertaining space was a simple gazebo-type structure with a thatched roof. Kathy, who had a beautiful view of the valley, added a large porch onto the front of their house, as a place to receive the people who came by. To create extra space for our visitors, we connected the new addition to our current home with a large breezeway.

The new construction had to be painted when it was finished, so we used this opportunity to change the color on the 'old' part of our house from red to off-white, while the painters were already there. These areas became such a blessing to us because it allowed us to maintain our own space, yet be able to welcome the many people who came our way in the hospitable manner that was expected of us. These additions also gave the kids a place to romp and play on rainy days, an easy-to-clean place to have birthday parties and an area for our workers to have their tea. I even hung up a porch swing out in the breezeway that I brought from the States. I didn't have a place for it when I brought it over to Kenya, so I was glad when I was finally able to use it. It brought back memories of home since it used to hang under the oak tree in my parents back yard.

Lesson Learned

Don't be disgruntled when your day doesn't go as you plan. Look at the interruptions as a way to try to be a blessing to someone who may need it more than you do.

House when first built & painted a brick red with white trim

House after addition, plantings and painting it off-white Lydia is standing on a brick path to the breezeway

TƏN

taman

(tah mahn)

*"A beautiful woman lacking discretion and
modesty is like a fine gold ring in a pig's snout."*
Proverbs 11:22 (TLB)

THƏ GRƏƏN MAN

Living in a developing nation makes you see poverty from a
different perspective. Poverty doesn't always translate into
unhappiness, like you might think. Some of the happiest, most
contented people I've ever met are the Kipsigis people; who by
the world's standards have virtually nothing. And, some of the
most unhappy, discontented people I've ever met are Americans, who have virtually everything and that, right at their
finger tips. Don't misunderstand me; in the big cities in Africa,
there are huge slums. One of the largest slums in the entire
world, with a population of a million people, is in Nairobi, the
capital of Kenya. Slums, wherever they may be, are filled with
such abject poverty and nightmarish conditions that it is hard to
believe that they are still around in this day and age.

People leave their families and their simple lives in the country for the allure of the 'big city' in hopes of better paying jobs or just a more exciting lifestyle. Much the same as Americans do when they try to 'make it big' in New York City or Hollywood, but then 'it' doesn't happen. In both cases, in Kenya and America, the person either runs out of funds to return home or doesn't want to return home as a failure. So, they stay where they are without the support of family and live in substandard conditions. Out in the country villages, families live in close-knit community, taking care of each other. Most have their farmland which allows them to at least feed their families, if nothing else. If they have the entrepreneurial spirit or an extra bit of land, they can take their surplus when they have it to market for a bit of cash.

No matter what their living conditions, I was always impressed with the grace and dignity in which the women especially, conducted themselves. The more I was around them, the more they reminded me of the virtuous woman spoken of in Proverbs 31. They rarely seemed to have a moment of leisure. From sunup to sundown and beyond, they were taking care of their families, homes, animals or fields. ("She watches carefully all that goes on with her household and is never lazy." vs.27-TLB) But unlike the Proverbs 31 woman, she and her household were not 'clothed in fine linens' (vs. 22).

Most of these village women had only two to three dresses to their name. One was for working in the fields and other dirty jobs, the second was for everyday use and the third (if they were lucky enough to have it) was for special occasions. Whatever the number of dresses, they were usually worn wrapped with a *kanga* to protect their dress. The *kanga* was also easier to wash and dry, and just to take care of in general. Clothing didn't have a lot of variety. Dresses were typically made of 100% polyester, with buttons running down the front from collar to waist (for easier nursing), with an elastic waist and pleated skirt (to fit more shapes and sizes) and stopped at mid-calf (for modesty's sake). Some of the fancier dresses would have a bit of a ruffle or lace or some other adornment.

Dresses were rarely thrown out. They were rotated from dressy to everyday, once it became damaged in some way. Then, from everyday to work dress, once it became ruined beyond repair. I would be amazed at times to see a woman working out in the fields in a frilly chiffon dress with ruffles and bows. But then when I got up close, I saw the stains or big rips in the garment that explained why she was wearing it for work. Day after day, month after month, season after season, year after year; these same clothes were worn until they fell apart and could only be used for rags.

The only concession for the weather was that a hip-length, belted cardigan was worn over the dresses. Most people, especially the women and children, went around barefoot with their shoes tucked under their arms as they walked to school or town. After they reached their destination, they would clean their feet by rubbing them across a stone or patch of grass, if a water pump was not available. Then they would slip on their shoes before walking inside. By doing this their shoes lasted longer. The majority of tasks were done shoeless, but with such poise that you hardly noticed they were barefoot. It was amazing how graceful the ladies could be while performing many tasks, but particularly when they climbed up and down wooden stiles.

Stiles are a ladder-type object used to straddle fences. Because of all the cows, which were allowed to roam freely, stiles were often preferred over gates. Many a woman could be seen balancing water or firewood on her head or a baby on her back, as she climbed these. I never quite mastered their graceful movements. Instead, I simply placed the object I was carrying on the top rung. Then, I climbed up one side and down the other; while keeping a hand on the object so it wouldn't fall over while I crossed over to the other side.

Lydia sitting on a stile that's about 4-feet tall

Most women and children wore simple canvas or plastic shoes. The more expensive leather shoes were reserved for the man of the house or the school children who needed to make the good impression for the family. Many country men wore shoes that have been made out of old tires. Tire shoes are seen all over Kenya and in many other African countries. What's left of the tire's tread is used for the sole of the shoe. Criss-crossing straps hold the 'shoe' onto the foot and are made out of the side portion of the tire. Rubber boots are another type of footwear worn by one and all. They were known as Bata boots because of the Bata Shoe Company that manufactured them. These ranged from tiny toddler-size boots in fun, primary colors to thick, black, clunky, heavy-duty boots for the working man.

In the bigger tourist towns like Nairobi and Mombasa where there is more of an international blending of people, women could be seen wearing just about anything. Trousers considered scandalous and inappropriate out in the villages were not considered quite so in the cities. Up until the 1940's, Americans felt that women who wore trousers were loose (of morals). Many Africans feel the same way today. Prostitutes will often wear trousers or a short skirt instead of a revealing top to attract men. This is done because the part of the female anatomy that African men find most alluring is the legs, especially the thighs. The breasts are seen as utilitarian because of breastfeeding and for that reason not particularly alluring.

Those strong feelings/opinions regarding trousers caused the missionary women to adopt the same mode of dress as the village ladies, when we were with them. We wore dresses or skirts and blouses most of the time, even inside our own homes, (at least while our workers were around). But come two p.m., when they left for the day, or during the evenings, or on our day off, we whipped out our shorts, pants or jeans to wear. Since we never knew when someone might drop by, we closed the curtains and kept a *kanga* draped over the back of the sofa for easy access if we needed to quickly cover up our 'inappropriate' clothing. When we went into Nairobi or on vacation in

Mombasa, we wore whatever we wanted and usually took the opportunity those occasions provided to 'glam-it-up' a bit.

If we wore any make-up, it was minimal and we wore very little jewelry; basically wedding rings and a watch. I was not sure what to do about my wedding ring because it was a diamond set and not a plain gold band. I also had a college ring I liked to wear, but felt guilty wearing rings on both hands when many women couldn't afford to have a ring on even one. For a time, I toyed with the idea of buying a plain gold band and leaving my diamond set back in the States with my mom. As a compromise, if we went to a new place or an area that seemed really poor, I would turn the diamonds and college ring into my palms so that just the plain gold bands were visible.

Many of these reservations about how to dress got cleared up one day after a conversation I had with a Kenyan woman out in the village. This lady was well educated and spoke English more properly than I did. This was a rare treat for me because most women spoke as uneasily in English as I did in Kipsigis, making our conversations rather stilted. Having this opportunity to speak freely, I asked her about the wearing of trousers, make-up and jewelry; along with other things. She confirmed that it was best for us to continue as we had been doing with the things we wore, except for the rings.

She said, "The achievement of going to university and graduating is something that many women dream of, but that few are able to achieve. I would wear your college ring with pride and explain what the ring is for if asked."

She then went on to explain about the wedding rings. "Men have to pay a bride price for the women they wish to marry by giving cows or goats to the bride's family. Did your husband have to do that?"

I replied. "No, that isn't the custom in America. We go on dates to decide for _ourselves_ who we wish to marry and then we just get married. Sometimes the man will ask permission from the girl's parents as a formality, but it's not required."

Looking at my wedding ring set, she asked, "Why do you have two rings?"

"This one," I said, pointing to the one with the bigger and smaller diamonds, "I wore when I became engaged; after Daryl asked my father's permission." I clarified. "This one," I said, pointing to the band with a matching small diamond, which made it a balanced set, "I received on our wedding day."

She nodded, putting her finger on the diamonds of the rings and said, "There are your cows! You wear your cows instead of having them out in the field." That made me smile and helped me in the future.

There had been times when the women had asked me how much Daryl had given for my bride price. When I had replied, "Nothing," they would act scandalized.

Later, when I was asked that same question, I would show my small diamond rings and say, "He bought these. They are worth many cows."

To this response they would nod their heads and grin, seeming proud for me that I was worth so much. I think they were amazed that I was the one that got to keep the bride price. The cows, money, etc. was always given to the bride's family for their use, not to the bride. And just like the lady from the village said, what seemed to make a bigger impression than the diamonds (because a bride price was expected) was the college ring I wore.

Even though the stone was synthetic and worth much less than the wedding ring set, it was what it represented that gave it such value. Most of the women I was surrounded by had very little, if any, formal education. It wasn't from lack of desire or intelligence, but from lack of funds. Education in Kenya was expensive for the average person. With funds being limited, the family had to choose who would be educated and who would not. So don't think that just because someone is illiterate, it means they are stupid. Most illiterate people of the world speak several languages, but can not read or write in any of them. I saw this proven time and again while we were in Kenya.

Lydia and I in our typical attire in the village

Since going to school was such a financial burden, most school-aged children wore their school uniforms in and out of school because this was all they had to wear. The uniform in the country, more often than not, consisted of a gingham or solid colored shirt for both boys and girls. The boys wore shorts or trousers with their shirts, while the girls wore a sleeveless, square-necked sundress on top of their shirts. Shoes were optional. In the big cities, the students were expected to attend class dressed in the complete uniform of shirts with ties, wool blazers with the school crest, knee socks and leather shoes. The only difference between the boys and girls attire was that the girls, again, wore skirts while the boys wore trousers.

Because of the limited clothing in most people's wardrobes, we decided to follow suit and wear the same outfits when ever we went into the villages. Because of the regularity with which we all wore our clothing, it became easy for us to recognize each other from afar. If you've ever wondered why missionaries dress the way they do, there's your answer. It's not that they have 'thrown in the towel' or have quit trying to dress nicely. It's just that with poverty all around them and people having very few clothes, the tendency was to downplay your clothing so that the clothes did not become the focus. After a while, this thinking begins to spill over to other areas and wearing the latest fashion just doesn't matter so much.

The outfit Daryl wore most of the time was khaki pants, leather tennis shoes and a collared shirt. I typically wore a blue jean or floral skirt, both of which held up well to dirt, a simple cotton blouse and canvas tennis shoes. We both carried a bag; Daryl a backpack and I, a big woven 'Kenyan' bag. In each of our bags we carried an English Bible, a Kalenjin Bible, a Kalenjin song book, a bottle of water, some toilet paper and a lightweight jacket or sweater. During the rainy season we carried umbrellas, rain slickers and wore Bata boots instead of tennis shoes.

Daryl usually carried extra Kalenjin Bibles and song books to either sell or give as a gift. I carried these store bought items as a hostess gift—a tiny package of KETEPA tea leaves, sugar (which was sold in a brown paper bag) and a small box of UHT—milk that needed no refrigeration. By bringing these 'fixings' for chaik, it enabled the hostess to provide refreshments for whoever came to the meeting; which would have been a great embarrassment to her and her family if she could not have done this.

One day as we were beginning our appointment out in the village, Lydia asked, "Are we going to the green man's house?"

"The green man's house?" I asked, confused.

"Yeah, the green man," she repeated.

Growing up in the South in the '60s and '70s, racial prejudice was an issue. We wanted to make sure our children had no such problem, so we never talked about the color of anyone's skin. The Kipsigis themselves only used three categories to describe people: African, European or Asian, so we followed suit. But, in none of those categories was the skin color green, so I assumed she was a little mixed up in her colors since she was only around three years old at the time.

Being that the majority of people in Africa have brown skin tones, I said, "Do you mean the brown man's house?"

She just emphatically continued, "No, the green man!"

"I'm not sure," I said, to let the matter drop.

This conversation took place as we sat beside the road waiting for Antony. We had a standing appointment on Thursdays at around 2 p.m. We drove the short distance to his village in Chebongi, visible from the town of Sotik, and parked at a curve in the road. If Antony was not there waiting for us, we would honk to let him know we were there and then wait for him to walk the short distance to the car. Antony would step out of his hut and wave to show that he had heard us. He would then go back into the hut to collect his things and say goodbye to his family before leaving to walk to our waiting car. As we sat there, we would watch his progress down the hillside, until he moved out of our view as he crossed the creek at the bottom of the hill.

The villagers had placed large stones at this juncture in the river to make the crossing easier. Since we traveled this same path with him before, we knew we would see him once he started back up the other side of the hill. After he reached the car, we greeted each other and then set off together to another village called Kapsogeruk. This village was just down the road a bit further by car, but would have been at an hour's walk.

The sound of our car served as an announcement to one and all that we were coming. All along the way, kids ran out to wave and yell, "How are you?" The English greeting they were all taught in school.

Or to yell, *"Wazungu, wazungu"* as we passed by.

Adults just raised their hands in a simple greeting, much like our own country folk do in the States. As we traveled, Antony kept an eye out and periodically told us to stop to pick up people along the way that he knew were headed towards the meeting. By the time we got to our destination, the car was packed full. We would all climb out of the vehicle, making sure we had the bits and bundles we had brought with us. Walking down the path to the hut from the road, the people who lived there, or those who had shown up for the meeting, would come pouring out to greet us. On the way to the huts, the hand shaking, greetings and introductions would begin anew.

As we veered off to go to the cooking hut to privately give the hostess the chaik making gift, the 'man of the house' stepped out of the hut. Imagine our surprise when we saw he was wearing a green shirt! Daryl and I looked at each other in disbelief and then down at Lydia in amazement. If she talked about a green man or any other color person after that, we didn't doubt her again.

Lesson Learned

You really shouldn't judge a book or a person by their 'coverings'. You need to take the time to look beyond the surface of both to understand them more fully.

Most women wear head coverings, sweaters, no shoes and babies tied to their backs. Most children wear their school uniforms and also carry babies (not dolls) on their backs.

eleven

taman ak agenge

(tah mahn   ahk   ah gehn geh)

"We share our mutual woes; our mutual burdens bear;
And often for each other flows the sympathizing tear."
Song: <u>Blest Be the Tie That Binds</u> by John Fawcett

OUR SECOND FAMILY

Breaking up the routine of work was almost always a welcome event. About once a month or at least every other month, the missionaries got together for a devotional, potluck meal, games and visiting. Being so far away from our own families back in the States, these events formed the missionary community into our second family. And just like we would with our families stateside, we got to show off our new additions, talk about our work or the newest things we found that made life a little easier and swapped out books and video tapes with each other. After these gatherings, we usually spent the night with a host family and in doing so formed a new or stronger bond of friendship in that way, too. Many times we took that opportunity to go to church with them the next day to see how they handled different aspects of the service, with an eye to try to copy it with our own churches. By doing the missionary 'monthly' meetings like that, it gave us a long weekend to be around fellow Americans and other teams from around the country. Since Monday was the day we typically used as our day off, we sometimes spent Sunday night in that different city if we could.

The monthly meeting weekend went something like this. On Friday, I gathered the food items together and prepared them as much as possible. On Saturday, I got up early to cook the food. Once it was cooked, it got wrapped in several layers of newspaper and towels to insulate it and keep it warm for the journey. Or, we would get on the road early to allow time to cook the food at one of the missionaries' houses once we arrived there. The potluck meal was eaten around noon after a devotional. Different ladies (usually the ones with older children) took turns teaching Bible classes for the kids during the adult devotional. This helped the parents by keeping the kids occupied during the devotional and getting the kids used to 'Sunday School' whenever they traveled to the US.

At the churches we worked with while we lived in Sotik, we didn't have a 'Sunday School', so our team appreciated those classes for the kids. When the village church services or meetings got long and the kids couldn't be still any longer, I would take them outside. (This was usually after sitting on a backless wooden bench for an hour or more. And, while trying to pay attention in a language that was not their mother tongue.)

Many times I was thankful for the respite myself. Spreading out my *kanga*, nearby in the shade, would put enough distance so the kids could quietly play, yet I could still hear what was going on in the meeting. Or, if they fell asleep, I would take them outside and sit beside them on the kanga. There were no 'nurseries' or other accommodations. The only place for them other than in my arms was the dirt floor of the school room or hut or the inside of our car. I would try to pick an inconspicuous spot at these times, but no matter where I went, one by one, other children came out, too. My kids were always a curiosity since *wazungu* kids were so rarely seen out in the remote areas we worked in. At times I felt like we were a carnival attraction because we would have a semicircle of kids sitting around us and whispering behind their hands as they stared and watched everything we did.

In hindsight, I wish I had brought along 'Sunday School' lessons or at least a picture from a lesson for them to color. Even if they didn't understand the English words written on it, the picture would have been treasured and proudly displayed. Not on their refrigerators, because they didn't have one; but on their walls like a prized painting. But, during the whole time I was with the Kipsigis people, my language skills were a struggle and I didn't want to be laughed at by small children, so I didn't do it. That was another reason why the classes provided for our children at these monthly meetings were so important. They got to be with other kids from their own cultural background and this helped them to feel more 'normal'. After the adult devotional and kids' classes were over, there was a time for prayer requests and announcements. While this was going on, the ladies made sure their dishes were on the table and ready to be served, if they had not done so already.

After a prayer, we ate our fill of wonderful American/ Kenyan dishes, served with chilled bottled sodas—Coke® for the adults and Fanta® for the kids. The adults sat outside on the lawn in chairs to eat our meal, with the kids at out feet. After the meal was over, the kids ran around and played games while the adults visited. Sometimes we started up a co-ed game of volleyball or some of the guys would go off to another teammates' house to play basketball. Usually, the ladies just stayed near the kids talking in groups, so we could keep an eye on the children while they played.

When everyone was finished eating, the workers for the team that hosted the event, would come out to eat before clearing away the food. It was fun to watch the 'shoe on the other foot' for a change. They would walk up and down the table of typical American potluck offerings, with plate in hand looking for some food they recognized. Usually, they skipped the casseroles all together. The Kenyans would pick foods that had rice and/or beans in it, dishes with plain meats, fruits they recognized or bread and a bottle of soda. If nothing was to their liking, they simply made a pot of chaik and some bread and butter sandwiches to eat while they washed up the dishes.

With paper plates and plasticware either being non-existent or exorbitantly priced; we used real dishes and silverware for the potlucks. Without our workers help, the clean up portion would have taken all day! Because they washed our dishes, pots, pans and utensils on a regular basis, it was easy for them to sort through all the dish and utensil patterns as they cleaned up. They also knew whose tables and chairs and other furnishings used for the day, belonged to which family. Again, because they saw these items almost daily and many times helped us to arrange it all on the host's lawn in the first place.

Missionary 'monthly meetings'—potluck style, accompanied with chilled sodas in glass bottles

One of the monthly meetings I remember well was one we attended soon after we first moved to Kenya. The city/team to host the meeting was in Eldoret and we were invited to stay with Beth and Monte Cox. Arriving at their home when the potluck and group visiting was over, Beth showed us to our room to put away our things. After doing so, I found Beth in the kitchen overseeing preparations for dinner. She asked how we were settling in since we had only been in Kenya a short while. After sharing we were currently without electricity, she told me she had dinner in hand, so there was plenty of time for me to take a bath before dinner if I wanted to take one.

At one time or another, everyone's electricity goes off and you need to heat water on a gas stove for a tepid bath. Without electricity, it was such a chore to take a bath because you had to heat up pans and pans of water and still, the bath wasn't very deep. It was just too time consuming to do more than have a shallow bath. More often than not, we re-used the water in the bathtub. I usually went first, while the water was reasonably warm, then Daryl would use the bath water after me because he could stand the tepid water better than I could. But more often than not, he just took a cold shower. Since water was an issue most of the time, we didn't pull the plug when we were finished taking a bath, either. We would use the bath water to flush toilets, change out the water in the diaper pails or the next morning Kipsang would use it to mop the floors or scoop it out and hand it over to Joseph so he could water the plants with it. Since Beth currently had neither electrical or water problems, I filled her tub to capacity with hot, steaming water and soaked and soaked! So she was correct in knowing how much I would enjoy a hot bath!

A short time later, Daryl knocked on the door to tell me supper was ready. I said, "Aaw, already? I'm not really ready to get out yet."

When he said, "Laurie, you've been in there for almost an hour." I got out, giving the tub one last wistful look.

It was hard to pull the plug and then watch all that lovely warm water spiral down the drain as I quickly got dressed. Coming into the dining room, I was embarrassed to find everyone seated and waiting on me. After the prayer, I noticed we were having Mexican food; complete with flour tortillas and corn chips. Oohing and aahing my way through the meal, I asked Beth where on earth she had gotten all the wonderful food. She looked at me a little perplexed and said she and her worker had made it. Explaining how everything was prepared, I realized I could do it, too. All the foods, except for one item, were easily available, even in Sotik! The one item I wouldn't be able to make for the time being was the corn chips, which we ate with homemade salsa and guacamole.

The making of the corn chips required a hand-held pasta maker that was only available in Nairobi. Instead of using wheat flour as you would for pasta noodles, you used *kimiyet*— a corn flour mixture. To make the chips, you dropped in a ball of *kimiyet* into the press. Turning the handle around the top of the pasta maker pushed a plate down, forcing the 'dough' to come out of the slots on the other end. But instead of having the dough drop into hot water like you would for pasta, we used hot oil like you would when you make French fries. The corn chips were done when they floated to the top. After scooping them out, you placed them on paper to drain off the excess oil and then salted them to taste. Yummy!!

Cleaning up afterwards, Beth patted me on the back and said, "I think you needed a break." She was SO right!

The first time our team hosted a potluck/monthly meeting, our guests were Amos and Anne Allen. I was thrilled to have guests. Anne and I talked and visited for a long time until she hesitantly mentioned, "It's almost six. Would you like some help with dinner?"

In the enjoyment of having guests for the first time in our new home, I had forgotten all about preparing supper. Since she had children, especially her small baby, Michael, to care for, I told her I would do it by myself. (I didn't have any children at that time.) It took much longer than it should have because I kept stopping to talk more with Anne. Finally, getting finished hours after I should have, we ate dinner. This taught me a valuable lesson in being prepared ahead of time for guests. In an area of the country that did not have ready-made foods or a grocery store filled with convenience foods, I needed to have everything in readiness so that I could visit with guests without stressing over it or trying to throw something together last minute without the proper ingredients. I was always prepared after that, with everything completely made or mostly assembled ahead of time. I even wrote out the menu and kept it nearby to help me to keep on task.

On another occasion when we went to Eldoret, we stayed with the Kehls. When we first came to Kenya, the Kehls were part of our team, but they later moved to the bigger town of Eldoret. The language spoken in the area around Eldoret (Nandi) is similar to the language spoken in the area around Sotik (Kipsigis). Since both languages are a dialect of Kalenjin it made the transition easier for them. It also made staying over for church the next day, after the monthly meeting, easier for us, too.

So far, the church service was progressing in a similar fashion to ours back in Sotik. When the children got fussy, I decided to take them outside. Susan took their son, Braden and went with me. Laying out a *kanga* to sit on with the kids, they soon settled down. One of them drifted off to sleep, while the other one filled their diaper.

Just as they started the song for communion, I had to leave to throw away the stinky diaper. After asking Susan if she would keep an eye on the kids, I went in search for a *choo*—outhouse, to dispose of the diaper since there were no trash cans. Being unfamiliar with the area, it took more time than I thought it would and I was gone longer than I had planned. By the time I returned, the church was quiet.

"Have they finished with communion?" I asked.

"Yes." She responded.

Feeling like I needed to set a good example, I decided to go inside and ask for communion. Village churches typically did not have communion trays. It was the practice in our area to pour a portion of juice into a single glass that was to be shared by all. The glass was then placed on a table at the front of the building so people could come up to take a sip of the juice for communion when they were ready. Or, if the group was large enough, someone would assist by passing it around amongst the participants. When everyone was finished, the last person (usually the person overseeing the communion) would drink down the remainder of the juice to 'finish it off'. This was done instead of throwing it out, which seemed wasteful to them, or pouring the juice that everyone had been drinking from in with the untouched juice in the bottle.

As I entered the building, I noticed a man standing near the front holding a bottle of juice in one hand and a glass of juice in the other. He looked like he was in the act of 'finishing it off', so I quickly walked up to him before he could do so. When I got up close to him, I told him that I had not taken communion yet. He looked at me with an odd expression so I repeated it again, saying the words slower and with panto-miming actions this time, "I...haven't...taken...communion...yet."

Instead of clarifying the situation, he continued to look at me with an odd expression showing me he did not understand. *"Great!"* I thought. *"He doesn't know English."* So with a sigh, I took the glass from his hand and drank down a portion. Then with a shrug, I went ahead and drank down the rest, to 'finish it off' myself. When I was done, I handed him back the glass and turned to leave.

As I did, Daryl and Kevin Kehl came into my field of vision. They too, had an odd expression on their faces. In fact, as I completely turned to face the entire congregation (of about fifty or so people), they were all very quiet, still and looking at me. Continuing on down the aisle and out the back door, I started to wonder if maybe I shouldn't have done what I just did. *"Oh well, I can't do anything about it now."* I decided.

Spying my *kanga,* I gingerly sat down so I wouldn't wake the kids who were both now asleep. As I was getting settled, the church began singing again. Just as I began to relax after the incident in church, convincing myself it wasn't as big a deal as I thought it was, Susan asked me, "What did you ask me before you went inside the church?"

Hesitantly and with dawning dread, I answered. "I asked if they had finished with communion."

"Oh," then a pregnant pause. "No, they hadn't finished. They were just getting started." She explained, having no idea what I had just done.

An actual church building built in a wealthier area

Embarrassment overcame me as I realized that instead of 'finishing it off' and looking like I was culturally aware, I looked like a complete idiot. I had drunk the portion poured out for the entire church! Thankfully, (when I had been up there in front of everybody) I noticed there was more in the bottle. So that no one would realize how mortified I truly was, I decided to go back into the building.

With both children sleeping on my *kanga*, I asked Susan if she could keep an eye on them while I went back inside for the rest of the service. (This was probably what she thought I was asking the first time I spoke with her.) When she agreed, I went back inside and acted as if nothing had happened in order to help cover up my faux pas. My idea seemed to be working. The now refilled glass was being passed around with the aid of the man from the front I had taken the glass from. A few people turned to stare; but we were always being stared at for some thing or other everywhere we went, so nothing was new there.

The glass slowly continued to make its way back towards the last bench where I sat and the whole incident seemed to have been forgotten. Whew! What a relief! The man from the front was now standing at the end of my bench waiting for the glass. Just as I was about to take the glass to pass it on, the gentleman in the aisle reached across me and grabbed it him self. After taking the glass from the person to my left, he passed the glass in front of me and handed it to the person on my right. I'm sure he did this so I would not take it and drink it all down again. How embarrassing! I guess I didn't cover it up as well as I thought I had.

With a few more words, songs and a prayer, the church service was over. I slipped outside to rouse the children and get them out of the way and to put the *kanga* and other items back into my big woven bag. As everyone left the building, we shook hands and exchanged pleasantries as we went our separate ways. *"Well that didn't seem too bad."* I thought, as the bulk of the group walked away. At this point, Daryl took the opportunity to slip away from Kevin and the other men, to walk over to me.

With a look of bewilderment he asked, quietly, but firmly "What were you doing? Why did you walk to the front of the church and then drink down that whole glass of juice?"

The embarrassment came back full force as I said all in one breath. "I don't know why I did that. I just knew I needed to take communion and he was about to 'finish it off'. So, I decided to step in and do it instead. I didn't know he didn't know English."

"Laurie, he does know English." Daryl said. "He was just probably in shock, like I was that you were taking the glass *out of his hand* in the middle of the communion service."

"I'm sorry. I just didn't know what else to do! I was trying to be a good example. I thought communion was over. I didn't know it was starting." I said, trying to sound pitiful.

"Well, please don't do that anymore. If that ever happens again, just wait until after services and I'll help you with it." He finished and then walked back to the other men.

Thankfully we were from out of town. So when the story was retold by the Kenyans about that crazy *mzungu*, who drank the juice for the whole church, I didn't have to hear it. Or, lose face with the Kenyans we were trying to work with. Among our own group of missionary friends, we often shared different mistakes or faux pas we had made whenever we got together. Telling these stories took some of the sting out of the embarrassment and helped us to be able to laugh about it. I think another reason we shared our stories was that it was a way of letting the new missionaries realize that mistakes happened to everyone. So, don't worry about it when it happens to you.

At our annual ladies' retreats I shared my embarrassing story about drinking the glass of juice. We all got a good laugh out of it and it quickly became a favorite. After that, I was often asked to tell 'The Communion Story,' as it came to be called, just about every year after that. For some reason they never seemed to grow tired of hearing it. The year we left Kenya to move back to the U.S., I was unable to go to the retreat. The ladies sent me a group picture and a little keepsake memory book since I couldn't attend. This memory book had other candid pictures from the retreat along with little notes of encouragement, prayers and memories from over the years. Several made the comment that 'The Communion Story' had been told for me in my absence during the time where we usually shared a difficulty we had encountered.

One of the ladies there, Becca Smith, even wrote, "We have made sure all of the new 'inductees' have heard your stories. Does that make you a legend?"

Well, I don't know if I would go that far. But that little book certainly made and makes me feel very loved and appreciated. I still look at it from time to time. There's nothing like being able to read nice things written about yourself when you're feeling a bit beat up by the world. Thank you, ladies!!

LESSON LEARNED

Most of the time, it's better to sit back, be observant and wait, then to charge in thinking you have the answer to the problem. If you don't, you never know how an impulsive act can take on a life of its own.

Women's retreat at the Rondo Retreat
centre, near the Kakamega Rain Forest
What an extraordinary group of women!!

TWELVE

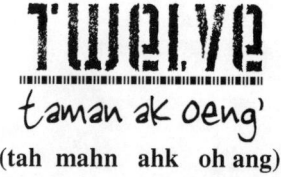

taman ak oeng'

(tah mahn ahk oh ang)

"What do you really want, Wyatt?"
"Just to live a normal life, Doc."
*"There is no NORMAL life.
There's just life...so live it!!"*
Movie: Tombstone

TAXI, AMBULANCE, HEARSE

Owning a vehicle is financially out of reach for most Kenyans. The number one mode of transportation is walking, seconded by riding a bicycle. Everywhere we went; people were walking alongside the roadways. As people heard the sound of our vehicles engine intrude upon their quiet walk along the country-side, it was like a trumpet heralding our arrival. Invariably as we approached, walkers would stretch out their arms with their palms facing downward. They then proceeded to flap their hand up and down at the wrist as we got nearer to gain our attention. This was the Kenyan equivalent of the American hitch-hiker's signal (a fist with the thumb sticking out), which means, 'Can you give me a ride?'

Our first vehicle in Kenya was a twenty year old army green Range Rover that had been used for safari tours down in South Africa. The ladies on our team called it the 'Green Tank'. I never feared driving out into the villages along badly rutted roads or up hillside terrain because that car really hugged the ground and could take us just about anywhere. Because vehicles are a precious commodity 'out in the bush', the men were called upon for their driving services all hours of the day and night. Hardly a week went by that someone didn't knock on our door (often at the wee hours of the morning) looking for a way to get someone to the hospital.

The person knocking at the door would have just spent anywhere from half an hour to hours walking to our home from their village in search of a ride. Most often it was because a woman in the village had started into labor and had reached a difficult time where things weren't progressing like they should. My husband disliked these 'calls' the most because by the time the man walked to our house, got us up and then they finally drove back to the village, the baby had usually been born. The mother, with her newborn child now safely nestled in her arms, was content to stay home and not go on to the hospital. There were a few times, though, where the bleeding wouldn't stop and the new mother went on to the hospital. He was glad to be of service, then, when it was really needed.

On other occasions where there was an illness and the person was too weak to move or walk, the men would get as close to the hut as they could so the 'patient' could be carried out by hand and placed in the car. The majority of the time, they arrived at the hospital in time to do some good. There were many times, however where people died in the car on the way to the hospital because they had waited too long to seek help. That was a traumatic experience for everyone involved. When this occurred, the group would continue on to the hospital so the individual could be pronounced dead by a physician.

If one of the missionaries was there, the body was released back into the family's care, which allowed the now deceased to be taken back home for burial. If the missionaries weren't there, the body was often put in the morgue so that the family would have to pay a fee (bribe) to get the body back for burial. Because of the fear of spirits around a body until it was buried, taxi drivers didn't want to carry coffins from the hospital to the villages. Those that did charged exorbitant prices to do so.

The very poor would often have to leave the bodies of their loved ones in the morgue until they were able to pay these ridiculous prices. Here again, we were called upon to pick up coffins from the morgue because people just couldn't afford to get the body home any other way. Sometimes, in order to try to get the outstanding hospital bills paid the hospital would keep the body until the debt was cleared. Or, the hospital could delay the release of the body because the coffin wasn't built or the death certificate wasn't ready. At times, this truly was the case. At other times, it was just another way to get '*chaik* money—a bribe' out of people. Most of these added 'fees' were often waived if one of us *wazungu* showed up. This was yet another reason we were called upon to help.

I say 'we', but really it was the men who had this task. I only did this once. I don't remember now why Daryl couldn't go. I think maybe he had malaria. But whatever the reason, I had to go in Daryl's place on the appointed day. He told me it would not be difficult because the coffin was already built, the 'fees' were paid, the hospital bill was paid, the body was to be taken to Chebongi (the village within view of Sotik) and the person's house was right by the main road. When any of those things were not in readiness, it could take hours or all day while you had to just sit around and wait. But, my only coffin carrying experience worked out exactly as Daryl said it would. I had rolled all the windows down thinking there would be an odor.

But all you could smell was the scent of the freshly cut wood of the coffin. Something for which I was truly thankful!!

Because there always seemed to be times that we had to sit around and wait for one reason or another, it didn't take us long to learn to carry a bottle of water, a snack and a book or notebook with us to help pass the time wherever we went. Some people carried extra aerograms with them and used the time waiting to jot off a letter to friends and families back in the States. I used to not bother carrying anything to do. Then after a long, rainy afternoon, that all changed.

One of the first times I went to a far away village with a new baby in tow, it began raining on the way there. By the time we arrived at our destination, the roads were a slippery, muddy mess. Knowing we were going to this particular location for a baptism and that it would take place down at the river, Daryl suggested I just stay in the car with the new baby for the hour it would take. I didn't want to sit in the car for an hour, but I didn't want to struggle through the muddy mess and possibly fall with a baby either. Taking the lesser of two evils, I waited in the car. The time passed quickly at first. Our baby, Lydia was capturing my attention with the typical care you give to babies; nursing, burping and changing a diaper. After she went to sleep and my hands were now empty, I quietly dug around in my bag for something to write with and on. I found nothing!

Frustrated, I took out every item and thoroughly searched them to try to find something to write with or on; still nothing. I squeezed up front and looked in the glove box and searched under the seats and floor mats. Eureka!! I found an orange crayon. Where it came from I have no idea, but I was glad to finally have something to write with. Now all I needed was something to write on. Climbing into the back seat, I turned around and looked at the cargo area one more time and saw the corner of a brown paper bag just peeping out from underneath the spare tire. I didn't have the keys to the vehicle to unlock the hatch back and I didn't want to climb over the backseat in a dress and try to move the tire because it might wake up Lydia. So, I decided to wait until she was awake before trying to dig it out. For some strange reason, it calmed me down to know I had this crayon and a brown paper bag to write on if I needed it.

Our first car, parked by the side of our house

Feeling more settled, I wondered what to do next. I didn't know where I was since I hadn't been to this area before. I decided I would just have to wait until someone came back to get me. Tired from the search, stress or simply from being a new mother, I lay down beside Lydia and made a mental check list of how this day could have been done differently. Before long, I fell asleep and woke up to the sound of the car doors being opened. Daryl and a man I didn't know climbed into the front seats glistening with rain. He told me he was moving the car to another location where we would be eating lunch so we wouldn't have to travel so far in the muddy mess.

As he was driving (sloshing and sliding) on the road, I told him of my search of the car and how I had gotten a bit stir-crazy while I had been waiting for their return. He told me not to feel so bad because it had been over three hours since he had left me, not the one he thought it would be. (I didn't have on a watch, so I had no idea of the time.) He went on to explain the events that had kept him from getting to me any sooner. When we finally got home after that long draining day, I resolved to make sure I was never without something to do or write on and with ever again! And, I didn't. No matter where I go, I keep a small note pad and pen with me to this day.

With things in Kenya being so much more primitive than in the States, I tried to be prepared for different scenarios and to avoid unpleasant situations as much as possible. So far, I had gotten around going to funerals. But one day, when we arrived at our usual appointment, we were told it was canceled because someone in the village had died and we were to attend the funeral instead. Walking a short distance, I knew we had arrived when we heard the singing, saw the crowd and the coffin. In a field, a short distance from the house, a grave had been dug and the coffin was resting beside it on something that looked like saw horses. The coffin was a plain wooden box like you see in the old westerns on TV. The lid had nails already partially driven in so it would be easier to attach the lid when it was time. This lid was lying on top of the coffin; pulled back enough so you could see the face and shoulders of the person lying in repose inside, if you chose to go to the coffin to look.

Sitting there I was thinking, *"This isn't bad at all. What was I so worried about? I'd like my funeral to be like this, just a simple wood box and singing outside on a beautiful day."* I sat there singing at the funeral of someone I didn't know and taking in the surroundings—the green grass, the fluffy white clouds floating in the blue sky and the warmth of the sunshine. But, the serenity of the moment was spoilt by the man standing at the head of the coffin. Whipping out a can of bug spray from behind his back, he sprayed it directly onto the face of the dead man in the coffin, making the flies scatter. Inwardly cringing, I tried not to show the dismay on my face and continued singing as if I was not shocked by the bug spray.

Focusing my attention elsewhere, the service eventually came to an end. The lid was put into place and the nails were pounded the rest of the way into the coffin. The sound of the hammer hitting those nails was just as jarring as guns being fired at a military funeral. Still, when I compare the Kenyan ceremony to the American ones, I prefer the simple way Kenyan services are conducted (minus the bug spray). Some thing about the whole American process seems so rushed. Just about the time you're letting the idea sink in that you're at a funeral—it's over. To Kenyans, death is just another part of the 'life' cycle; in the same manner as birth, becoming an adult and marriage and needs to be duly noted, not rushed.

One year there was an outbreak of spinal meningitis that seemed to primarily affect our area of the country. There were hundreds of deaths. And just like the first time I went to a Kenyan funeral, many of the village meetings were changed to funerals instead. Almost every day for a time there; one of our three men had the duty of transporting the body to its burial site. It was a scary time because after the onset of symptoms, most people died within a few days or within 24 hours. Even though the person was dead, the virus was still 'alive'. The meningitis virus could still be caught by those handling the body, which brought even more fear than usual to the families involved. Knowing our Kenyan brothers and sisters had no other options during that critical time, our men continued trans-porting the bodies. None of the women did.

Out of concern for the live virus in the dead bodies that our men were transporting, Brenda Vick contacted someone she knew at Tenwik Hospital. Tenwik was an American funded and partially American staffed bush hospital that was about one and a half hours away over dirt roads. She told them our husbands were transporting people who had died from the meningitis outbreak and asked if there were any precautions they should take. The person she spoke with said for us to all come on a certain day and time for a vaccine. But, we were told not to tell a soul they had the serum. If we did, she said it would cause a riot because there wasn't enough for everyone who wanted it. The vaccine was being saved for the hospital workers and people like us who had more exposure than the average person. As directed, we showed up at the hospital without telling anyone what we were doing. When our turn came, I was not allowed to have a shot, or injection as they called them, because I was pregnant. I was told that at the first sign of symptoms, I was to come in immediately. Thank goodness I never needed it!

Our cars' services were needed for other things, too. Everywhere we went throughout the country, whether we knew them or not, we were flagged down by people wanting rides. If we were in 'our' area we filled the car to capacity, plus. We were a bit more discriminating outside of our area simply because we could not communicate with them to know where they wanted to go. We would start out on our journeys into the bush with our kids in their car seats. If we needed to take them out to make room for another person, we always did. The car seats were put in the back and the kids would sit on my lap or someone else's. Our generation grew up not even using seat belts. Car seats for children were unheard of. Because of this, we opted to take our kids out of their car seats when need be and would say a quick prayer for their protection. Traveling on a dirt road, we generally didn't drive that fast and we rarely had much traffic to contend with. Whenever we were on paved roads driving faster and around other cars, we were usually heading out of town and by ourselves; solving the car seat problem.

For Daryl's birthday one year, I had a big wooden box built for the tire changing tools that usually slid and bounced around in the back. These tools were huge because the Range Rover is such a large and heavy vehicle. This new tool box stretched from tire wheel to tire wheel and was also used for additional seating. A lot of the time, the kids we picked up and our own children (when they got older), would climb over the backseat and into the cargo area to sit on the tool box as their seat when they gave up their place for another person. Occasionally when we would leave a village with the car already packed with people, I opted to sit in the back on the tool box with our kids because it was roomier. Even full to capacity, people would still flag us down to try to get a ride. Often times, the younger people in the car would get out (without being asked) and finish the journey on foot so that an older person or a woman with a baby or a person carrying a heavy load could have their place in the vehicle.

As we were driving down the road one day, we noticed Antony holding up his right hand in an **O** shape by having his fingertips touch his thumb. Then with his left hand flat, he bumped the **O** of his right hand onto the palm of his left hand a couple of times. People, who had just had their arms out to flag us down for a ride, immediately dropped them and continued on their way. After seeing him do this a couple of times, with the same results, we asked him what he was doing to get the people to drop their arms like that. He told us it was the symbol for 'full to capacity' or 'no room'. We were glad to learn this. It was nice to have a way to show people we were too full to pick them up and that was why we didn't stop. Not because we didn't care about their plight.

After a while, people began to recognize us by our car. They also figured out we took Mondays as our day off. Even when we drove into the nearby town of Kericho, a town about thirty to forty-five minutes away (depending on the conditions or disrepair of the road), we would come out of a store to find someone leaning against our car so they could get a ride. We enjoyed shopping in Kericho because it had a grocery store with some pre-packaged items, canned goods, fresh fruits and vegetables, fresh milk, UHT milk by the case, sodas by the case, packaged flours, rice, pastas and some packaged cheeses and meats. They also had cleaning supplies and a much wider selection than anything we could find in Sotik.

Kericho also had other stores where you could buy fabrics, shoes, lanterns, seeds, furniture, paints and all sorts of different items in a limited assortment, but there nonetheless. It also had a movie theatre, where mainly East Indian films were shown. Occasionally, Americans films came to town and we would go to watch them on those rare occasions. There were also car repair places, a place to get your hair cut, places to eat out, a library and a golf club. Since we seemed to travel to Kericho so often for things, we tried to move there once but couldn't find enough available housing for all of us. We could only find one or two places that were acceptable. Since we didn't want to leave a family behind we decided to stay put in

Sotik for a while longer. Surprisingly, for a town the size of Kericho, it really had a lot to offer. I always felt like I had stepped back into civilization whenever we went there. I often wondered how different our lives would have been if we had moved to Kericho in the first place instead of Sotik.

If we needed to plan a trip to another city to get or do something that was not available in Kericho, we learned not to speak openly about it in front of the Kenyans (if we wanted some alone time). If we didn't, then the next thing we knew, we had a carload of people coming along with us, which defeated the purpose if we were trying to get away. Many times when we picked up people along the roads, we would mistakenly assume they lived nearby. When the 'lift' seemed to be taking longer than we anticipated, we asked them how much further it was to their house or village. I don't know why we bothered to ask because we got the same responses every time we asked. We were either told, "Just there." or "Notfah—Not far." I'm sure all trips seemed 'notfah' or 'just there' when going by car as opposed to by foot.

Usually I didn't mind carrying people from one place to another. It was something I could easily do whether I knew the language well or not. People just had to sit and point in the direction they wanted me to go and I could take them there. When they wanted to stop, they would bang on the side of the vehicle to let me know this was their stop and wanted to get out. No speaking was even required for that. I think taking people places lessened the guilt I felt about the luxury of owning a car in such a poor country. Many times when I saw a woman bowed down under a heavy burden she was called upon to bear—water, wood, a child or all three—I would think, 'There but by the grace of God, go I.'

Be that as it may, we still got the urge, now and again, to just take a break and get away from the people we were surrounded by 24/7. Going into Kericho with all it had to offer was still in the Kalenjin area. Because of this, we liked to go to into Kisumu, a large town to the north of us, about two hours away. Kisumu was about three to four times the size of Kericho with three to four times the amount of people, shops, things to do and places to eat.

But where we liked to go the most while in Kisumu was The Sunset Hotel, because we could do so many things at one location. If we gave the kitchen staff a few hours notice, they would make us up a huge order of *chepatis*. A *chepati* is a type of flat bread that is a cross between a flour tortilla and pita bread. If we wanted a large amount of fifty to a hundred chepatis, we would drive to the hotel first thing to place an order and then do our shopping. There was no other place where we could get 'ready-made' chepatis, so we took advantage of this opportunity whenever we could. We froze the *chepatis* for quick and easy Mexican meals and casseroles or to make simple cheese pizzas.

Even if they did not have the time to make this special bread, there were lots of other foods from the menu for us to choose from. Those foods were nothing special. They just seemed so because they were served outdoors by the pool. Since Kisumu was at sea level not up in the mountains like our town of Sotik, it made the temperature about fifteen degrees warmer and great for swimming year round. And to top it all off, the pool was situated in a lush garden that gave a panoramic view of Lake Victoria.

We felt very rested after a day in Kisumu. The kids were so exhausted from having swum all day that they went straight to sleep at bedtime with no fuss, which was always a plus! I had gathered all kinds of foods not available in Kericho giving variety to our usual meals. Plus, we had a nice meal out in a vacation like setting. But I think the biggest perk of all was knowing we wouldn't run into anybody we knew. We could truly let down our guard, be our American selves for a change and even wear shorts if we wanted to. It was a great time had by all and one we liked to duplicate as often as we could.

Lesson Learned

A vehicle is more than just a way to get from point A to point B. It is a luxury to be appreciated; for most people in the world, to own a vehicle is only a dream.

Daryl, Steven (a few months old) and Lydia
(2 1/2 yrs old) enjoying The Sunset Hotel pool.
The city of Kisumu is beside Lake Victoria

THIRTEEN

taman ak somok
(tah mahn ahk so moke)

"Since the Lord is directing our steps, why try to understand everything that happens along the way?"
Proverbs 20:24 (TLB)

HEAVEN TO HELL IN 60 SECONDS

Daryl was going to a men's retreat and the rest of our team was either on vacation or getting ready to leave on furlough. So for one reason or another, I was going to be in Sotik all by myself with a three year old and an eleven month old. I didn't relish that thought so I called up a friend in Kitale, a town six hours to the north of Sotik, to see if I could stay with their team while our husbands were at the men's retreat. Susan Hayes was a friend I didn't get to see much because of the distance, but we worked it out so that I could go. Elizabeth, Brenda Vick's nanny/language helper, somehow heard I was going to Kitale and asked if she could go, too. Since she spoke English so well and could help out with the children it sounded like a fantastic idea to me. So, I said she could come, having no idea how blessed I would be to have her with me on the trip.

Roadways in Kenya are infamous for their despair. The stretch of road between the two large towns of Eldoret and Kitale were especially bad. The traffic between those two large towns flourished with a number of *lorries*—trucks and over-crowded taxis. The taxis—*matatus,* were actually single cab trucks with a tall covered back enclosure. The tail gate was removed and replaced with a door to allow passengers easier access in and out of the matatu at the designated stops. Because the roads were so eroded and in such disrepair, vehicles typically drove down the center of the road when there was no oncoming traffic. This was done to try to dodge the worst of the potholes and the fraying edges of the tarmac—pavement.

Having finished my visit in Kitale and now headed back towards home, I myself was driving down the center of the road because it was surprisingly empty. Noticing an approaching vehicle, I eased back over onto my side of the road. Because the road was so eroded at this juncture, the front wheel slipped off the tarmac. This was a common occurrence so I was not overly concerned. When the back tire on the same side also went off the tarmac onto the narrow dirt shoulder, I still was not worried, even though I was now driving at an angle.

For miles behind me and in front of me, this portion of the roadway was raised about five feet above the fields and sometimes barren stretches of land it was surrounded by. A huge drainage pipe had been laid crossways underneath the tarmac just ahead of me. When I noticed the dirt around the pipe had either not yet been replaced or had eroded, so that the dirt shoulder I was now precariously driving on was about to play out; that was when I began to worry.

Finally, the oncoming vehicle passed me so that I could go back into the center of the road again. In my hurry to do so, I did what you've been taught NOT to do. I stomped on the brake and sharply turned the wheel to quickly get all four wheels back onto the tarmac. It worked, but not for long! One second I was fishtailing on the road, and then the next I was in a cloud with a tinkling sound like wind chimes. I didn't remember passing out or even closing my eyes. But I remember opening my eyes, seeing the haze about me and thinking, *"I'm in heaven. That was so quick and easy. What was I so scared of?"*

When I heard someone crying out in despair, I realized that didn't fit, so I must not be in heaven after all. About that time the cloud, which was actually dust that had gotten stirred up when we went off the road, began to dissipate and I could see that I was still in the car. Watching Elizabeth crawl out of the car and hearing her cry out reminded me I was not alone. Why weren't the kids crying? I turned around to look into the back seat to see how the children had fared and why they weren't making any noise. All I could see was the bottom of the seat. I whipped back to the front thinking, *"I've killed my babies. I'm in hell!"*

In sixty seconds I went from thinking I was in heaven to being in hell. I sat there vacantly staring in despair wondering how on earth I was going to tell Daryl I had killed our children. My vacant stare finally took focus and it was then that I saw the pedals in front of my eyes. What were the pedals doing there? While I sat there, trying to figure that one out, I felt a drip hit my hand. Looking down to where my hand was resting, I saw the ceiling light. Why was the ceiling light between the seats? Finally the fog in my brain cleared and I put these oddities together to figure out that the car was upside down. Maybe the kids weren't crushed after all!

Gathering my courage, I turned to look through the seats again, this time bent over at the waist, looking upside-down. I can't describe the joy I felt when I saw the kids still strapped into their car seats. Steven was hanging upside-down in his car seat, which was still securely buckled into the backseat. Lydia was right-side up in her car seat. Her chair had come loose, flipped around in the car and had come to rest tilted partway out the broken window. They both looked unharmed. But neither had opened their eyes or made a sound which concerned me.

While I sat there wondering why they weren't crying, another drop of fluid fell on me. According to all the movies I'd seen, we needed to quickly get out before the car exploded into a fireball. Seeing Elizabeth standing outside the car next to Lydia, wailing in despair, I called to her to get Lydia out of the car. She immediately quit wailing when she realized we weren't dead. I don't even think Elizabeth bothered unclasping the buckle of the car seat. She just reached in through the broken window and yanked Lydia out. When she cried out at being so rudely awakened, it was music to my ears.

To get to Steven, I crawled through the two front seats noticing the broken glass that was everywhere as I did so. More fluid dropped onto my back as I passed through the seats. This time I noticed the fluid had an oily smell rather than the gasoline smell I feared. Positioning an arm under Steven, I unlocked the car seat and caught him as he fell out. When he made a little grunt upon contact with my arm, I was thrilled to realize he was also alive. Clutching Steven to me, I crawled out one-handed to see Elizabeth holding Lydia, who was now awake.

Elizabeth calmed down when she realized we were all alive and not dead like she first thought when she had crawled out of the car and started ulalelling. (This African cry of despair was what I had heard when I was coming to in the cloud from the accident and realized I couldn't be in heaven.) Standing next to them I assessed the damages. Elizabeth, though shaken by the experience, seemed untouched. Steven was now awake and also seemed no worse off from having just been in a car accident. (Unbelievably, he and Lydia had fallen asleep in their car seats about thirty minutes before the accident and had stayed asleep through it all.) Looking at Lydia, I could see she had blood dripping onto her shoulder from a cut on her head just above her ear. Usually, I freaked out at the sight of blood, especially on my children. But, knowing there was no one else around to attend her, I applied pressure to the area by pulling her against me and keeping my hand over her wound. We all just stood there, looking at the Range Rover. It was upside down with the wheels in the air, still ever so slightly spinning. Every piece of glass was broken out, which accounted for the tinkling noise I had heard earlier, when I thought I was in heaven. (I don't know what made me pass out. I didn't have any cuts or bumps on my head to indicate a head injury. But apparently Elizabeth stayed awake for all of the accident because she said the car flipped several times before coming to rest on its roof.) As we continued to stand there taking it all in, seemingly from out of nowhere, people started to arrive.

Elizabeth said, "We need to get the valuables before they are stolen."

I looked from Steven in my arms, to Lydia clutched to my side and then to Elizabeth in confusion and said, "I have everything right here!"

Feeling that I was not understanding, Elizabeth said, "Your purse and the suitcases and the groceries."

Letting go of Lydia's head, I looked at her wound. Thankfully, the cut was only superficial and had already stopped bleeding. It may have occurred when Elizabeth yanked her so roughly through the broken window, but I don't know that for sure. We walked over to the other side of the Range Rover, picking up cans and odd bits that had been flung from the car and put them in a pile. Seeing my purse, I picked that up and put it on my shoulder.

"Now what?" I thought.

No sooner was the thought expressed then up drove a policeman *in a car*. A very rare sight let me tell you! Most policemen traveled by bicycle or by foot. He questioned me in the Kiswahili language, which I didn't know. I called to Elizabeth to translate for me, who had been standing guard with the kids and the items we had collected from the Range Rover.

They began carrying on a conversation without me, with Elizabeth answering what she could. When she didn't know how to answer something; she asked me. I would answer her and then she would translate my English into Kiswahili for the officer. All of this took place while I stood guard, over to the side, with our suitcases and the kids. At one point, the officer asked to see my Kenyan driver's license.

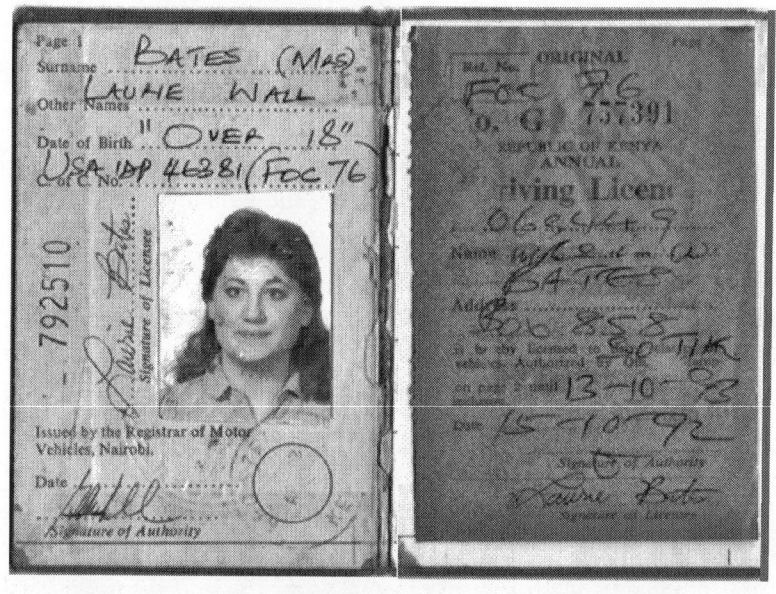

NOT shown in actual size, this license is a tri-fold,
document. It is four inches tall and stretches
out to over a foot in length when fully opened

As I dug through my purse, I realized I must have forgotten it at home. But I did I have my American license with me. (I preferred to show this when asked for identification, instead of carrying around my passport.) Taking it out of my wallet, I handed it to him expecting to hear a reprimand. He didn't say a thing. That amazed me. (I found out later, that as long as I had a valid driver's license from my own country, I didn't have to keep a valid Kenyan driver's license, too.) The questions continued in much the same manner; with Elizabeth answering on my behalf until she needed to ask me something and then she would translate my response when need be.

Then, the conversation seemed to become a little heated which surprised me. The Kipsigis people go to great lengths not to show anger. But then, I thought, *'We're not in the Kipsigis area, maybe that's why he's acting differently. Since he is a police officer, he probably has to be firm or even show anger when dealing with some people.'* But we had been cooperative, so I didn't understand why he was talking to Elizabeth like that.

Finally, she said, "They're flipping over the car."

"Flipping over the car?" I asked, wondering how they could do this out in the middle of nowhere.

"Yes, step back." She instructed.

Elizabeth and I took a few steps away from the vehicle, taking the kids with us. The officer called out something in Kiswahili which caused the crowd which had gathered, to move to one side of the vehicle. The officer began counting in Kiswahili. Before my astonished eyes, I watched as they worked as one to lift up one side of the vehicle and push it over. The weight of the vehicle and the momentum flipped the car right side up again. I was quite impressed! A slogan often used by Mzee Jomo Kenyatta, the first president of Kenya was, *'Harambe—Let's Pull Together!'* It was amazing to see those words put into action.

The movement of the vehicle had stirred up another small cloud of dust. As it cleared, everyone walked over to the flattened vehicle to take a closer look. Going to the driver's side, with Steven in my arms and Lydia holding onto my skirt, I reached through the window to take the keys out of the ignition so they wouldn't get stolen. As I did so I realized the car, unbelievably, was still running. Surprised, I went ahead and turned the car off, putting the keys in my pocket. At the same time that I was doing this, the officer was walking around the vehicle and talking with Elizabeth. She shook her head as she answered which seemed to anger him. Tilting her head towards me as she answered again, it seemed like she was saying, '*If you don't believe me, ask her.*'

It must have been something to that effect because they both walked over to where I was standing with the children and Elizabeth said, "He wants to know where the other people are."

"Other people?" I asked. "What other people?"

"He can't believe that the car looks this badly and that no one was killed. He thinks there were others; but that we are afraid to tell him about them." She explained.

Shocked, I shook my head 'no', held up four fingers, pointed to the four of us and said, "Four; just the four of us."

Finally satisfied, he took more information and said something to disperse the crowd. With Elizabeth's help again we talked about what to do with the car. We decided to have it towed to the police station, where hopefully it would be safe. Telling us he had paperwork to fill out, he got into his car and drove away; leaving us behind with the wrecked vehicle.

"We can go now," Elizabeth said, as we watched everyone go their separate ways.

"Go? Go where?" I responded, looking around at the now empty scene. There were no huts as far as I could see and all the people had left. I thought, *"Now what are we going to do? How will we be able to carry groceries, suitcases and Steven?*

He was only eleven months old and not yet walking. I had learned to tie my children to my back with a *kanga*, just like the African ladies, but had not brought one with me on the trip, so he would have to be carried to wherever we were going. The accident had occurred at the halfway point between Kitale and Eldoret. I didn't know if we should start walking back towards Kitale, to the Hayes' house, or to go towards Eldoret which was on the way to Sotik. Just as we scrambled up the embankment with our stuff, a *matatu*—taxi pulled up and stopped in front of us. I couldn't believe it! The *matatu* had "Eldoret Town" written on a sign placed on the dashboard. Problem solved! We were going to Eldoret.

The sign was there so people would know the *matatu's* final destination. The *matatu* started out its trip in the town of Kitale that we had just come from. It had probably stopped all along the way, picking up and dropping off passengers until it had come to where we were. Giving the suitcases and battered box of groceries to someone to tie down on the top of the truck, we climbed into the back. Another surprise awaited us as the door was opened and we climbed inside the *matatu*. Usually, these vehicles were packed to overflowing. This one only had a few people so we wouldn't be crowded at all. What a relief!

As we settled into our places in readiness for the trip to Eldoret, Lydia noticed a bag of chips in my purse and pulled them out. Helping her open the bag, I saw the dried blood on my fingers. The *matatu* seemed unusually quiet, so I looked up into the faces of the other occupants, only to see them all staring at me. They start peppering Elizabeth with questions so I went back to what I was doing. After giving the bag to Lydia, Steven squealed, grabbing at the bag of chips. I took one of the chips out and gave it to him, making him happy.

The people laughed at that and said, in Kalenjin, "*Lagok kerege*—Children are the same!" We all laughed, which seemed to put everyone at ease for the remainder of the trip.

Arriving in the town of Eldoret, the driver delivered his passengers at the main taxi hub in the center of town which was crowded with people. I asked Elizabeth to tell him that I would pay him if he would take us directly to a friend's house. He agreed. As the driver parked beside the Conway's house, I saw

Hollye step out of her house with a confused look on her face. She was probably wondering why a *matatu* had driven down her driveway and stopped beside her house. Her face cleared as she watched us climb down out of the back of it. What a bedraggled sight we must have been.

Hollye slowly walked up to our little group taking us all in. Putting her arm around me, she calmly and sweetly said, "It looks like you've had a little trouble." I could have cried with relief to have such a kind, understanding person to talk to. After telling her I'd rolled the Range Rover in between Eldoret and Kitale she said, "Then we'd better get you to the doctor."

"I just don't think I can face the crowds right now!" I said miserably, thinking of our hospital back in Sotik and all the stares we usually encountered.

"What if I call a private doctor I know? It's after hours but I think he would open up for you if I explained the circumstances," she continued.

"That would be wonderful!" I exclaimed with relief.

"Why don't you go wash your hands and faces while I see if he's available?" Hollye suggested.

What a Godsend that doctor was! I had him check out Elizabeth first while I stayed with the children. I was a bit surprised when she came walking out with a cloth neck brace. The doctor said Elizabeth told him her neck was sore so he gave it to her as a precaution. She was to wear it for a few weeks to be on the safe side. When our turn came, the doctor allowed me to continue holding Steven as he checked out his head and neck. When he realized Steven was not upset, he asked me to lay him down on the examining table. He ran his hands over Steven's extremities, making sure nothing was swollen or bruised. When he began to push on his stomach, I asked him what he was doing. I was stunned when he said, "Looking for internal bleeding."

Thankfully there wasn't any. He repeated this process on Lydia and then me. The doctor spent a few more minutes looking at the cut above Lydia's ear, which hardly even showed now that we had washed away the blood. He told me to gently, but thoroughly wash everyone's hair because our scalps were full of tiny bits of glass. The doctor then gave me some children's liquid pain reliever, instructing me to give everyone some, including myself, before going to bed that night. He said not to be surprised we woke up with nightmares because of the accident. When I explained they had been asleep through the whole ordeal, he still suggested we take it to help everyone to relax and get a good night's sleep. (He was right. The kids cried out in their sleep and I kept having weird dreams. When they woke up, I gave them the medicine and took some myself. We all slept fine after that.)

On the way back to the Conway's, I told Hollye what the doctor said. She made arrangements for Elizabeth to clean up and stay with her house worker who was a female and lived close by. Hollye then suggested that I start giving the kids baths while she worked on supper. I was astonished at all the sand-like glass particles I found when I drained the tub after each use. As I washed and dried each of the kids, I ran my hands over them in much the same manner the doctor had when he examined them. Once again thanking God for their sound, uninjured bodies.

After the kids were dressed for bed, I went to the kitchen to ask Hollye if she could watch them while I did the same for myself. Instead, I found her husband, Larry, who was now home from the same men's retreat Daryl had gone to. Hollye must have filled him in on everything because Larry didn't ask me any questions. He just gave me a hug and told me he would keep an eye on the kids for me while I got cleaned up. It was wonderful to be so nicely taken care of. As we ate dinner, I received the call from Daryl I had been waiting for.

Our accident occurred in February of 1992—years before cell phones were introduced to Kenya. Because the land lines are so unpredictable, it is reported that 1 in 3 Kenyans now have cell phones. They have to walk into town and pay a fee to charge them since they don't have electricity. Several reports have stated that there is a race on to see who can come out with the first phone that will charge via a tiny solar panel on the back where the battery usually goes. When they do this it will capture an even bigger market since so many people in the world do not have electricity. It's hard for me to wrap my mind around a person sitting in a mud hut, or other primitive conditions, talking on a cell phone. But, I definitely see(and saw) the need for it.

The bright red, cloth covered driving license of EAK which stands for East Africa Kenya.

Two other countries in the 'East Africa' group are Uganda – EAU and Tanzania – EAT

Before leaving for the doctor's office, I placed a call to the guest house where Daryl was to spend the night. I left a message asking him to call me at the Conway's house when he got in. Quickly, I told him about the accident and asked him how soon he would be able to get to Eldoret. He told me he wouldn't be able to come until the next day. Daryl reminded me that he was staying an extra day in Nairobi after the retreat to see the Vicks off at the airport for their furlough.

He was then to drive their truck back to Sotik for them. With all that we had been through that day, I had forgotten all about that. I was disappointed when I realized he wouldn't be able to get to us until much later than I had hoped.

The next day the Conways had scheduled to go on a trip with another family. Telling them not to change their plans for us, Larry and Hollye made sure we had everything we needed before they left. Everything seemed back to normal. The kids were playing and arguing over Andrew Conways' toys. Elizabeth was resting and hanging out with the Conway's worker. I was in the kitchen, getting us something to eat, while we waited for Daryl to get there. Opening the upper cabinets to get out a glass, I couldn't seem to make my head look up. Placing my palms on either side of my neck, I pushed up my head. This unnerved me a bit, but it was a minor thing in comparison to being able to walk away from a vehicle that had rolled several times.

When Daryl arrived at the Conways, he gave everyone hugs and kisses. The kids went back to their playing and we settled down to talk. As I relived everything that had happened, I began to cry. I hadn't realized how much I had held my emotions in check for the kids. But now that Daryl was with us, I was finally able to just let go. I cried even more when Daryl told me that the Vicks said we were welcome to use their truck while they were away on furlough. Repairing a vehicle in Kenya was often a lengthy process if the part was not available and it had to be imported. I hadn't even thought about how long it was going to take to repair the Range Rover. Having the Vicks truck would make that whole process so much easier.

Later that afternoon, we left the kids with Elizabeth so we could go to the police station. Daryl had me take him to the exact spot where the accident had happened so I could go over how it had all transpired. After that, we drove to the police station to see if there was anything further we needed to do. The police officer wanted to charge us a ridiculous amount to have our car towed to Sotik (really just a bribe). Since the engine still worked, Daryl decided he would drive it the short distance to the Conways house to see how it handled. I followed slowly behind him in the Vicks' trucks. We both traveled with our flashers on.

Arriving at the Conways, he said the Range Rover handled just fine, but that it was difficult to drive since the roof was touching the headrests. In order to see, he had to drive hunched over with his head partially sticking out the window. Once there, he used a winch to pull up the roof a bit so he could drive it without being hunched over. Daryl drove the car home to Sotik with the rest of us following behind in the Vick's truck. He caused quite a stir as he went down the road in a squashed Range Rover with all the glass broken out of it. Elizabeth and I shared a few giggles at the double-takes people gave as he drove past and then at the expressions we saw on their faces.

When I got back in my own house I was finally able to think more clearly. I was overwhelmed with the many ways God had been with us throughout the whole ordeal. *First,* the vehicle flipped several times, but we were able to walk away from it (even when neither Elizabeth nor I were wearing seat belts). *Second,* shortly after we were all out of the vehicle, a policeman just showed up. Believe me, that was a gift from God. *Third,* I had Elizabeth on the trip with me and she was able to serve as a translator. *Fourth,* no sooner had we finished with the policeman than a *matatu*-taxi pulled up to give us a ride. *Fifth,* there were only three people inside instead of the usual ten, giving us plenty of room and time to catch our breath. S*ixth,* the driver agreed to take us right to the Conway's door, instead of having us walk which was what was normally done. *Seventh,* the accident happened in an area where there were people that I knew instead of in another part of the country where I didn't have friends. *Eighth,* there was a private doctor for us to see after hours, instead of the busy hospital where we would have been the brunt of a lot of stares. *Ninth,* the Vicks leaving on furlough which made their vehicle available to us at the time we would need it the most! All of these things made me feel truly blessed and under God's care and protection. But the thing that I appreciated the most about the accident was that it took away my fear of death. In the blink of an eye, or a flip of a car, you can be in heaven before you even realize what is going on.

This thought was brought to truth about two years later. One of our missionary family's in Meru, the Searcys, suffered a bad accident. On a routine drive out into the village, Bill swerved to miss an animal in the road, something we all did from time to time. The vehicle went out of control and flipped, just like mine did. But, Cathy, the wife and mother to three small children, was thrown from the vehicle and badly injured. She had to be taken to Nairobi for treatment along with their son D'Abraham who had gotten pinned underneath the truck when it came to a stop. Bill and the other two children, Joshua and Esther were treated for minor injuries and then released from the hospital. Cathy wound up dying from her injuries and a memorial service was held for her in Nairobi, before she was taken for burial in the U. S.

Their accident, so similar to mine, made me question God as to why I was spared when Cathy was not. I struggled with that for some time. Finally, I had to quit wrestling with it and asked God to help me with my feelings. I derived a lot of comfort from the verse I used at the beginning of this chapter. It still gives me comfort when things in life seem unfair and I can't figure out the 'why' of it. It reads: "Since the Lord is directing our steps, why try to understand everything that happens along the way?" (Proverbs 20:24 TLB) God is not asking us to put our faith in Him only when things are going our way or when His requests seem logical. Sometimes we just can't comprehend at all why he is having us to go through some of the things we do. But that's okay as long as we don't let it put a wall between us and God. If it does, we need to tear it down—bit by tiny bit, or with one mighty shove. We just need to get rid of it. If we don't, the one who suffers the most is us.

LESSON LEARNED

We know that God always cares for us. But when we see it right before our eyes it's very humbling to know how much He loves and cares about us.

Picture taken in conway's driveway after Daryl winched up the roof so he could drive the vehicle to sotik

FOURTEEN

taman ak ang'wan

(tah mahn ak ahng wan)

"What's your word? Shoo? That it? Shoo?"

"Shoo!! Shoo!!" [Herd of water buffalo scatters.]

"That's a fine word you got there, Baroness."
Movie: Out of Africa

TRIPS TO THE MARA

There was a 'back way' into the Maasai Mara Game Park from our home in Sotik that shaved at least an hour or two off of our trip. With our close proximity to the park we liked to take visitors there whenever they came. Our first chance to go with no one to guide us was when my sisters, Carla and Teddie, came to see us. It was also our first time to try out the tent we had bought from the Chownings when they were packing up to leave Kenya to move back to the States. This 'back way' into the park was a series of twists and turns on dirt roads. At times the 'road' was little more than a footpath, or just a grassy plain. When we eventually drove up to the Talek Gate of the game park to pay our entrance fee, Carla said in amazement, "I thought for sure you were lost and just didn't want to admit it! There were no road signs or markers, just rocks and trees."

Slowly, with many stops to take pictures of the varied wildlife, we made our way to another gate of the park called the Sand River Gate. This gate had a designated camping area and was near the lodge where we were to have dinner. When we arrived at the campsite, there was nothing that distinguished the camping area from the rest of the park except for some circles of rocks that were blackened from numerous campfires. Simple wooden barracks the park rangers lived in were a short distance away. But, they blended in so well with the surroundings, you hardly noticed them. I assumed the presence of man, guns and fire was enough to keep the wild animals at bay.

Setting up camp didn't take long. We only put up the tent while it was still light; leaving the rest of our things in the Range Rover so they wouldn't get stolen while we ate dinner at the lodge. Driving the short distance to Keekorok Lodge, we cleaned up in their generously appointed bathroom and put on dressier clothes while we waited for the time that dinner was to be served. It was worth the effort. We were served an elegant three course meal on china complete with linen tablecloth, silverware and candlelight. It was quite the civilized affair out there amongst the wildness of Africa. After dinner, we played cards in the lounge area near the fireplace. When we all started taking turns yawning, we decided to head back to the tent. No matter how luxurious our surroundings were, it was time to go. (We again, used the lodges' bathroom to change out of the dresses and heels we had put on for dinner, into the clothes we were going to sleep in.)

As we drove from the lodge to the camping area, the only illumination to navigate by was provided by our vehicle and the moonlight. In a moment or two, we made out the headlights of an approaching vehicle. As we got closer, he flashed his lights at us, which in Kenya meant he wanted us to stop. We slowed down and stopped beside his parked vehicle. The man behind the wheel was a game warden.

He asked us a bit angrily, "What are you doing driving out in the park after dark? It's illegal to drive after sunset!"

Daryl explained that we were camping at Sand River Gate and were coming back from dinner at Keekorok Lodge. After hearing our explanation, he allowed us to continue on our way, but with the reprimand not to do it again. Daryl parked the car with the headlights facing the tent so we could put the remainder of our things in the tent and get some sleep. One last thing we did before zipping the tent shut and calling it a night was to use the 'bathroom'. Since it was pitch black with not another soul in sight, we just took a few paces away from the tent and that space became the 'bathroom'.

Finally, we were all in and settled down for the night. Off in the distance we began to hear the sounds of the African plains, waking up instead of quieting down like we were. We heard the zebra making a braying noise like a donkey, the eerie laugh of the hyena and other sounds we couldn't quite identify. One sound we all knew well was the roar of the lion. When one roar sounded very clear and louder than the others, Carla said, "I think I'll just sleep in the car." Asking for a flashlight and our keys, she did just that.

The next time we camped at 'The Mara' was with an experienced camper and hunter, Wes Miller, a deacon from our overseeing church in Muskogee, OK. As we drove around the park this time, Wes had us stop to pick up firewood along the way. When we pitched our tent this time, it was Wes, Daryl, our kids and me. Upon reaching the campsite, Daryl and I set up the tent while Wes built a fire with the wood he had collected during our drive. Sitting around the fire, we ate a simple meal of sausage balls, boiled eggs, carrot sticks, fruit, cookies and drinks. While we ate, we asked Wes to give us some tips about camping since we didn't have much experience.

He told us a bucket was a very useful item to have on hand because you could do so many things with it. You could use it to hold the wood you picked up along the way. It could be inverted to use as an impromptu seat. Later, you could haul water to douse the fire when you broke camp. He went on to tell us more helpful things and about some of his camping and hunting experiences. I was so exhausted from getting up early, keeping the kids entertained on the long and bumpy trip and from getting things set up that I could hardly keep my eyes open. I called it a night, taking the kids with me. After getting them into their beds, we fell asleep almost immediately.

Lydia was three years old and slept on a cot. Steven, who was ten months old, slept in a portable crib. (This campout was one month before the accident where I rolled the Range Rover.) Daryl and I shared an air mattress and Wes used sleeping bags. All in all, we were pretty comfortable. During the night, the sound of a light rain hitting the tent woke me for a second, or two. When I realized it was not a rainstorm and we wouldn't need to seek shelter in the car, I was lulled back to sleep. The next morning the kids couldn't wait for breakfast at the lodge, so I had them nibble on leftovers from the night before as we sat by the remains of the fire. While the men worked on breaking down the camp, they told me about the 'visitor' we had during the night.

Wes too, had heard the 'light rain' hit the tent, but he knew it wasn't rain. Being an experienced hunter, he recognized it as the sound of leaves hitting our tent as they fell off the tree under which we had pitched our tent. Shining his flashlight out the 'window' of the tent, where he lay sleeping, he saw our very large visitor, an elephant. Wes said he looked at the distance between our tent and the tree and then the distance between the tree and the Range Rover. He figured if the elephant wanted the bigger area to pass through it would be the area between the tree and the tent. Thinking the area where he was laying would be the most vulnerable; Wes moved his sleeping bag to the zippered door area of the tent. Waking Daryl who was sleeping soundly by then, Wes whispered, "We've got company, BIG company!"

They laid there quietly watching the elephant rip out leaves from the tree above us with his trunk, carry them to his mouth and then, slowly chew. After a bit, he lowered his trunk, turned around and lumbered off, away from the tent, tree and car; slipping off into the night as quietly as he had come. Sitting there listening to the guys talk made me realize the fragility of our situation. This sturdy canvas 'house' could have been easily whisked aside like a fly if the elephant had chosen to pass that way. And to think, the kids and I had slept through it!

Later that afternoon we stopped at a different lodge before exiting the park to stretch our legs, let the kids burn off some energy after being cooped up in the car all day, use the bathroom facilities and try to cool off a little in the shade. At that time, vehicles in Kenya didn't come with air-conditioning as an option. All the other times we had gone to Maasai Mara had been during American summers, but Kenyan winters, so the temperature had been cool. This time, in January, it was America's wintertime but one of Kenya's hotter months. The frozen water from the day before was now melted and tepid. It was wet and soothed our dry throats, but not much more than that.

When we met back up at the vehicle, Wes said, "Hey, I saw people in there drinking sodas from a bottle. Let's get some to take back home with us."

"They're pretty pricey out here," Daryl said.

Knowing the high price was more for the glass bottle then its contents, Daryl dug around in the Range Rover until he came up with four bottles. Wes and Daryl headed back into the lodge with the bottles while I got the kids back into the car and buckled into their car seats. After a short wait, they came out with big grins and cold bottles of sodas. After they too resumed their seats, we began our journey back home. They told me that at first they didn't want to give us the bottles. But, after Daryl showed them the empty bottles and spoke a little bit of Kalenjin and Kiswahili, they relented because they could tell we lived there and were not tourists.

"How much money was that anyway?" Wes asked.

"About a dollar and a half," Daryl answered.

"That's not bad at all," I said. "That's not much more than I pay at home."

"Not for all of them. They were a dollar fifty each." Daryl clarified.

"Oh, that was expensive. Wes, you didn't need to do that!" I said, thinking how we paid a quarter for each soda in Sotik.

Wes took a big drink of his cold Coke® and said with a sigh, "I wouldn't have cared if they were five bucks a piece. I still would have bought'em!"

We all laughed at that and took a sip. I don't know if a soda ever tasted as good as it did then. That cold Coke® in that chilled bottle was definitely refreshing. The adults sipped at theirs to make them last. Lydia hugged her Fanta® to her, but shared sips through a straw with Steven.

Our next outing was easier in some ways because we had lived in Kenya longer. On that drive we relearned something that we had grown complacent about because of our growing familiarity with it. Wildlife is called wild for a reason, it is unpredictable. That trip to Maasai Mara was made up of three missionary families. There was our family of four, Dave Vick and his son, Josiah and the Trull family. Rick and Marinda Trull with their two sons, Jeremy and Travis, were getting ready to move back to America and wanted to see the infamous park before they left. They lived in Meru which was about ten hours from Sotik. The nearest park gate to us in Sotik was about four hours away. Being closer to the park than they were, plus knowing our way around a bit, they asked if we could accompany them. With there being ten of us, we traveled in two vehicles.

Traveling together in Kenya was not too difficult because there was not the vast interstate and roadway system that criss-crosses America. If one of the kids needed to take a 'potty break' or we needed to stop for some other reason, the car at the back would flick their lights. We learned to do this type of signaling from the Kenyans while we lived there. Once in the game park, we flicked the lights and pointed in the direction we saw animals. Since this was in a time before cell phones, it worked well and effectively to communicate our needs.

At one location, we all got out of the vehicles to look out over a river embankment called Hippo Point. This is a bend in the Mara River where animals, especially hippos, tended to hang out because of the easy access to and crossing of the river. (This site is famous for the Wildebeest migration which crosses the Mara River at this spot.) The congregating of animals also brought the crocodiles and tourists. Just like the sightseers, we pulled over to take a look and pictures at this scenic location. There is a pathway down the side of this embankment where you can cautiously walk down to get a closer look, right to the river's edge. Two of the boys, decided they'd rather have a snack than go down to the river. I volunteered to stay with them while Daryl took our kids, now about three and a half and one and a half years old, for a closer look.

The two boys were standing on the seats with their head and shoulders out of the sunroof, eating from a plastic bag filled with sausage balls while they watched baboons frolic in the nearby trees. Taking this opportunity to get out and stretch, I took a moment to appreciate the beauty around me and to tell myself, *"You are standing in the middle of the Maasai Mara Game Park. Standing where the wild animals roam free and where just over there in that river, there are crocodile!"* A movement out of the corner of my eye broke me from my reverie. Turning back to the trucks to check on the boys, I saw them throwing food toward the baboons.

"Boys, don't do that!" I shouted. "Those monkeys will come inside the truck to get to the food," I continued, pointing to the trees.

As if on cue, several baboons started heading our way. The boys threw the bag to the ground, dropped down inside the truck and latched down the sunroof so the monkeys couldn't get into the truck. I turned towards the pack, clapped my hands, waved and shouted, "Get! Go away!"

The combination of shouting, clapping and waving from a human turned them back to the trees. Satisfied, I bent down to pick up the bag of sausage balls. Noticing that the bag was only a little dusty and that the food inside was okay; I decided to put it back in the truck. Turning to do so, I saw a big male baboon still headed in my direction. Thinking to trick him, I turned around and went in the opposite direction, behind the vehicle. Passing between the vehicles, I was pleased with how I had outwitted him. But as I turned the next corner, there he was.

I had forgotten about the bag of food in my hand until he lunged at me to get it. That surprised me. But instead of dropping the bag like I should have, I held on to it because I was thinking, *'This is food I made for my kids, not for you. You can't have it!'* So, I kicked out at him and loudly said, "NO!"

Again as if on cue, the guys this time came running up out of the embankment, shouting and waving their hands. Picking up stones, they threw them at the big male baboon until he went all the way back to the trees. Rick Trull and Dave Vick got to me at about the same time asking, "Are you okay?"

Surprised at their quick entry onto the scene at just the time when I needed them the most and at their marked concern for me, I said, "Yes, I'm fine."

By that time, Daryl was there too, carrying Steven and Lydia; accompanied by Marinda and their other son. Everyone was out of breath. I was surprised because they all seemed to be so worried about me. Since we were all now back at the trucks, we decided to get in and see more of the park. As we separated to get into the various vehicles, Josiah Vick said, "Wow, Aunt Laurie, I didn't know you could scream like that!"

"I screamed?" I asked in surprise, as I looked into their faces for confirmation.

"Yeah, really loud!" he exclaimed which made everyone laugh and broke the tension I now understood. Here I thought I had been calm, cool and collected in the way I had handled the big male, baboon, when in fact I had been screaming like a banshee! No wonder the guys came running up out of the ravine at just the moment I needed them.

"What happened?" Marinda asked as we climbed into the truck and continued on our way. After I told her about the boys and the bag of food, Marinda, who was a nurse, asked, "Did he bite you?"

"I don't know. I don't think so." I replied, as I began to pull up the leg of my jeans to take a look. I was surprised to see there were some scratches and a bite mark just above my knee.

"It doesn't look like he broke the skin," Miranda said. "So, you should be just fine." She got her first aid kit and cleaned the scratches with alcohol, rubbed on triple antibiotic ointment and then bandaged it to be on the safe side.

As darkness approached, we pulled up to the lodge's parking lot. This time, not only were we eating there, but we were sleeping there, too. What a luxury to bathe the dust off, eat a fine meal and then sleep in soft beds for the night. The reason we could afford to sleep at the lodge this time was because the U.S. dollar had a good exchange rate. It was nice not to go camping, for a change.

The last time we went to 'The Mara' was when my sister, Carla, and her family along with our parents, came for a visit. There were eleven of us all together so we had to go in two vehicles everywhere we went. By that time we had lived in Sotik for about 5½ years and had acquired a second vehicle, a Subaru station wagon. The Range Rover had also been replaced with a Toyota four-door Hi Lux truck just like the rest of our team used. (The Range Rover was totaled in the accident I had.)

With kids coming along and me staying at home with them more often, we thought it was a good idea to have a second car for times when the men were away and we didn't have another vehicle on the compound. That way, I or one of the other ladies on the team, wouldn't be stranded if ever an emergency occurred. Or, if one of the kids got sick and needed to be taken to the hospital. (There were no doctor's offices. If we needed to see a doctor, we had to go to the hospital or clinic to see one.) The Subaru also came in handy as a back-up vehicle if someone's car needed to be repaired. We used these two vehicles to go into Nairobi to collect Carla's group and to do things in the area that didn't require a four-wheel drive vehicle. The game park was definitely an area where we needed a truck, so we traded vehicles with the Vicks and set off to see some animals.

Since our excursion into the game park began on a Sunday morning, we stopped at a village church on the way to Maasai Mara. As we walked from the vehicles into the school for services, I was amazed to see how dry and cracked the soil was in that area. While we were inside having our church service, a light rain fell. Even though it was a short rain, it was enough of an impact to close up the cracks in the soil. When we passed that way again hours later, I wondered if I had imagined it, until someone else in our party commented on it, too. After eating lunch with the church, we got back on the road to resume our trip.

The area we were driving on was not 'the back way' into the park that we usually took, but a nice paved road, with hardly any traffic on it. Trying to make up some time for the lengthy service and because the road was such a nice one, Daryl was driving fast. I was driving at a quick pace myself, but he still managed to get a little ahead of me. Even though he was now out of sight, I was not very concerned because there was only one way to go. If there happened to be an intersection or a place where we needed to exit off of this road, I knew he would stop and wait for us there.

Approaching a big curve in the road, I slowed down because I could see some cattle crossing up ahead. Seeing those cattle made me nervous. A week before, we had gone into Nairobi to collect my family. The morning of their arrival we had gone to the memorial service for Cathy Searcy; the missionary who had died in the car accident when they swerved to miss an animal in the road. With this fresh in my mind, I took my foot off the gas pedal to slow down, but was hesitant to apply the brake. Just as I got close to the cattle, a calf was startled by the vehicle and instead of continuing on with the rest of the group, it turned back and ran right into me.

We had been instructed not to stop whenever there was an accident because of 'mob justice'. We were told to continue onto the nearest police station and file a report once we got there. Being unfamiliar with the area, I didn't know where the nearest police station was and I couldn't go looking for it because then we would become separated from Daryl. I didn't know what to do so I just drove on, feeling awful about it. After a short while, I found Daryl pulled over waiting for me. I flashed my lights and honked my horn to let him know I needed to talk when he started to drive off again. I hopped out to tell him what had happened, while the rest of the people in my truck got out to talk to the others. Daryl assured me I had done the right thing and further explained, to me and everyone else in the party, that it was the farmer's responsibility to keep the cattle off the road and the fault did not lie with me.

There had been some discussion among our group of turning back to try to find the owners and to make restitution for the calf. Daryl said it would be difficult to do this because he probably wouldn't be able to communicate with the owner since we were now in a different tribal group and we didn't know the language. Plus, the owner would not want to come forward because he wouldn't want to pay the fine that would be levied at him for not keeping his livestock off the tarmac. We resumed our trip, but I still felt bad for having injured and possibly killing the young cow. The accident made me feel a little nervous about driving, but thankful that I was driving our truck and not the Vick's truck, since the collision broke a headlight

About two hours later, we left behind the nice paved road and were making our way on a dirt path. We pulled to a stop beside a wide, deep ditch that was crossing our path to get a better look. Because of the light rain we had earlier, it had a good amount of water in it. Getting out, Daryl and I looked it over discussing what to do. In doing that, we saw another crossing a short distance away. Daryl decided to go down there to cross. That way, if one of the trucks got stuck in the mud, the other truck would have more room to maneuver to pull it out. As a precaution, Daryl manually locked in the four-wheel drive on the tires before attempting to cross. The Vick's truck, had a metal shell on the back of it like the *matatus*-taxis did. With this metal shell and our luggage, it made their truck much heavier than ours and therefore, more likely to get stuck.

While Daryl was getting the Vick's truck ready to cross the ditch, I backed up a short distance and told everyone to get a good hold onto something because we were crossing the ditch. Revving up the engine, I gunned it. This shot the truck down, across, up and over the ditch in one fluid motion with water and mud spraying out as we crossed. Getting to the other side, I put the truck in park to wait for Daryl and his crew to cross over.

While we were sitting there, my dad who was in the front seat with me, burst out laughing and said, "I never would have imagined my sweet little Laurie driving like that!" He continued chuckling and gave me a pat on my shoulder to show he didn't want me to take offense at his words, which I didn't.

About thirty minutes after the ditch crossing, we began to see lone wild animals outside of the Game Park and everyone began to get excited. An hour after that, we came up to one of the gates for the park. After we were inside the park for a bit, my brother-in-law, Ricky, asked if he could drive. Forty-five minutes later, I asked him if I could resume driving again. I was pregnant with our third child, Lee and for some reason, being the driver instead of the passenger, lessened the nausea.

The exchange rate was still in our favor, so we stayed at the Keekorok Lodge again. We arrived in time to unload and relax a bit before dinner. My mother couldn't believe that such lovely accommodations would be waiting for us at the end of such a bumpy, dirty trip. After dinner, we broke into small groups. Some played cards; some watched the video playing on the TV about the animals that could be seen in the parks of Kenya, while others simply relaxed in the main lodge by the fireplace. I was overly tired from the long day and bumpy trip. Because I was, I started feeling nauseous again. So, I told everyone goodnight and went to the room taking our kids, Lydia now 4½ and Steven 2½, with me. While the kids and I were in the room, Daryl made arrangements with a game warden to take our group out just after dawn, but before the breakfast buffet opened.

When the early hour rolled around, some of the group decided the bed was just too comfortable and decided not to go after all. That was a shame because the game warden knew well the 'stomping grounds' and habits of the animals under his protection. Within a short period of time, we saw a large variety of animals. After breakfast, we retraced our drive to see if the animals were still there so the rest of the group could see them. Almost all of them still were! What a treat.

Lesson Learned

Take time to enjoy the simple pleasures of life when they come your way. Just because something is simple does not mean it's not worthy of your time or appreciation.

A pride of lions sunning themselves on an outcropping of rock in the early morning hours just after sunrise

FIFTEEN

taman ak mut
(tah mahn ak moot)

"I'm so glad we had this time together, just to have a laugh or sing a song. Seems we just get started and before you know it, comes the time we have to say, So long."
Song: <u>Carol's Theme</u> by Joe Hamilton

VISITORS TO KENYA

The first of our families to come visit us were two of my sisters. Carla, who lived for a time in Norway and had explored Europe while doing so, was a seasoned traveler. My younger sister, Teddie, a high school family and consumer sciences teacher, was getting married later that year at Thanksgiving. Since I would be almost eight months pregnant at the time of the wedding, I wouldn't be allowed to fly internationally. So I was thankful they had decided to come together to visit us. Having only been in Kenya for about ten months, we weren't exactly sure what to show them. We decided to let them see how we spent our time doing day-to-day activities and to do some 'touristy' things we had only heard about but had not yet found the time to do. One of the first things we did was to take them out to our weekly meetings in the village so they could get a taste of African life, both literally and figuratively.

At one of those meetings, there was a baptism in the near-by river. To get to the river we had to walk down a steep hillside. Since these tended to be lengthy affairs, we would then sit or stand as the baptism took place. Being as there were no TVs or 'entertainment' out in these remote places, anything out of the ordinary drew people's attention. Because we inevitably drew a crowd, these occasions were used to evangelize the 'neighborhood' and we would include a riverside service with the baptism. On our way back up the hill to the village, I realized I was getting acclimated to the elevation because my sisters needed to stop to catch their breath fairly often, whereas I didn't. Another thing that showed me we were beginning to fit in better than I thought, involved a chicken. It was funny how things that never happened to you before would tend to happen when you had guests.

When the Kipsigis could afford it, they would build a separate cooking hut from the sleeping hut. The cooking hut would have a grass roof to allow the smoke from the wood fire to slowly dissipate. This extra hut also gave more sleeping space for their ever growing families. If they could afford it, the other hut, used for living and entertaining would have a corrugated metal roof. I didn't like these roofs as well, my own house had one. I much preferred the picturesque grass roofs, but the Kenyans said the upkeep on a corrugated roof was simpler. Plus, you had the extra bonus of being able to catch rain from off of a corrugated roof that you didn't have with the thatched roofs.

Most African compounds used every square inch to serve double-duty or multiple purposes. Like the roof serving as protection from the elements and to catch rainwater. Flowering bushes were planted around the perimeter of the hut for décoration, a bit of privacy and as a place to lay your clothes to dry.

The fire pit was used to boil water, cook food and give off heat. The smoke from the fire had an additional benefit in that it helped to keep out mosquitoes—always a bonus in an area where you needed to fight malaria.

The area we were taking them to for their next meeting was a poorer area so both living and cooking spaces were under one roof. Walking into the hut through the one outside door, you entered the main living area. That space had a small table with a couple of chairs and a couple of benches. The fire pit, where the family's meals were prepared, was over to one side. There was generally one other doorway on the inside of the hut that opened into a smaller room that held two single-size cots. This doorway often had a wool blanket tacked onto the doorframe instead of an actual door. Probably to save on the space a door would take up in such a small area and because it was cheaper, more easily obtained and transported.

The smoke from the cooking area could be so over-powering at times, it made your eyes water. Because of the smoke and the crowd that was expected, the doorway to the sleeping area had been draped open. When more people arrived for the meeting, my sisters seized the opportunity to move to the sleeping area to be near the window and to get out of smoke. I went with them, to try to act as an interrupter. Little did we know there was a territorial hen whose nest was in the corner by the door.

Sitting there, visiting and drinking our chaik after the meeting was over, the chicken jumped into the open window that my sister, Teddie, was sitting in front of. Startled, she turned to see what had made the noise. As she was turning, the chicken used this little bit of extra space to jump down out of the window. Flapping its wings practically in her face on its way past her, it landed at its nest, where it settled down. It didn't cause anymore problems but it left Teddie with a feeling of unease, which was understandable. Walking back towards the car after the meeting was over I told them, "That has never happened to me before!" (And it never did any other time after that either.)

Later that evening, my sister Carla and I were doing the dishes after supper and reviewing the events of our day. Carla confided in me while we were alone by saying, "Teddie said she doesn't know how you can do this all the time. She doesn't think she could."

I was a little surprised by that statement. The evening before, Teddie had told us some things that had happened at the low socio-economic high school where she taught in the Baton Rouge area. She told how she had to get in the face of a boy much taller than she was to get him to settle down and do the assignment he was given. (Being only five foot two, it wasn't very hard to find someone taller than her.) She also told us about a fight that had broken out at school where a desk had gotten picked up and thrown.

Thinking about the conversation from the night before, I replied, "That's funny. I thought the same thing last night when she was telling us about her job." I then thought to myself, *'Better a flying chicken then a flying desk any day!'*

We crammed all we could into the short time they were here. We ate lunch at The Tea Hotel in Kericho where you could eat a good meal out on an open air verandah that overlooked and was surrounded by tea fields, hence the name. I took them to the nearby town of Kisii, famous for its Kisii Stone. This stone, when soaked in water, became softened to the point that it was easy to carve. Because of this characteristic of the stone, it was also known as Soap Stone.

Soap Stone or Kisii Stone's natural hues of off-white, pink, tan and gray, could be solid, speckled or swirled variations of these colors. All kinds of things were carved out of this stone, but the most popular items were chess boards, candlestick holders and animals. I thought its natural colors were beautiful, but I've also seen this stone with black or red shoe polish rubbed into its surface so that further embellishment could be carved onto its now altered facade. I once saw a Scrabble Game made out of soapstone in Nairobi. I didn't have enough money on me at the time to purchase it. I wish I had because my family enjoys playing Scrabble. That would have been a unique board game to play on and a nice memento.

We also went camping in the Maasai Mara Game Park, souvenir shopping in Nairobi and ended our trip by traveling to Mombasa by overnight train. Mombasa is an old seaport town. Because of its easy access to the beautiful Indian Ocean, it has become a popular resort town, too. Carla Dean, a single missionary lady living in Nairobi, suggested a restaurant near her house where we could pick up some 'take-away' food to eat on the train. After eating our food, there wasn't much else to do. It was pitch black outside, so we couldn't enjoy the scenery. We tried to play cards in the compartment but the cards kept sliding around with the constant and uneven motion of the train, so after a while we quit playing. The four of us settled on passing the time by singing church songs in three-part harmony until the porter came to convert our bench seating into beds.

The back of the vinyl coated 'bench' was lifted up and held into place with a chain on each end. A 'net' was secured across its length to keep the occupant from rolling out at the stops. The 'bed' was a couple of thick wool blankets, then a sheet to give a cushion against the hard vinyl and then a sheet and two more wool blankets to cover yourself with. Somehow, these six layers were folded all together to make a zipper-less 'sleeping bag'. A pillow completed the 'bed'. Though these beds were surprisingly roomy and comfortable, we didn't get much sleep with all the rocking and the occasional stopping and starting of the train.

But, all discomfort was forgotten the next morning as the new day was dawning. Right about the time the dark was displaced with the first rays of sunrise; the train was traveling though the Tsavo National (Game) Park. This portion of the railroad was made popular by the book, *The Man-Eaters of Tsavo* and the Hollywood film based on it called, The Ghost and the Darkness. (Those were the names given to lions by the British, East Indians and Africans building the railroad.)

Stories were told of how these two, maneless, mail lions almost kept the Kenyan-Ugandan Railway from being built because they had developed a taste for human flesh. Instead of stalking wild game, they attacked the men as they slept at night, which were much easier prey. There were reportedly over 100 victims. Eventually, the lions were outsmarted, tracked down, killed and made into floor rugs, enabling construction on the railroad to resume. Years later, the rugs were sold to the Field

Museum of Natural History in Chicago, where I believe they are still on display today.

But, decades later, as you peacefully laid there on your bunk, you could look out the big picture window that took up most of your compartment and view the wildlife—mainly gazelle, zebra and giraffe. There was some quality in that moment while you watched the animals going about their normal activities on the African plains that made you appreciate them and want to protect them in this, their unique habitat. Before too long, a hut here and there, some abandoned, some occupied, started to crop up; then villages and small towns replaced the animals all together.

As we began making the descent into Mombasa, which is at sea level, the air began to feel humid and hotter. Stepping out into the corridor, we opened the window to catch a breeze and view the downward snaking path of the railway, until finally, we were in Mombasa. From the moment your feet touched the station platform, you were practically hounded by porters trying to help you with your bags or find you a taxi to take you to your destination—'for a small fee.' Carla, Teddie and I stood guard over the luggage, shaking our heads no to those who came our way while Daryl went out to negotiate with a driver over the fare. And just like the constant motion of the train was for-gotten as we got to enjoy traveling through Tsavo, the pestering of the porters and the heavy congestion of the traffic was put aside the moment we saw palm trees, white sand and the beautiful aqua water.

While at the hotel, we booked a small handmade canoe called a dhow. For an hour, the guide had us gliding over the beautiful clear water of the Indian Ocean, pausing now and again over a sandbar so that we could see the marine life below. It was a time we remember fondly. We repeated many of the same activities, four and a half years later when Carla came for another visit to Kenya, this time bringing her family and our parents. With the seven of them and the four of us, it was a large group for me to plan for, but I think an enjoyable time was had by all.

Carla, calling in preparation for the trip asked, "What is the current exchange rate?" When I told her it is seventy shillings to the dollar she says, "Did you say seventeen?"

"No, seventy," I repeated.

"Seventy shillings!" she exclaimed, "I was reading my notes from the last time I was there and we got sixteen shillings to the dollar. I can't believe the exchange rate is so good!"

And indeed it was. We got to do lots of fun stuff for the two and a half weeks they were there because of the good exchange rate. Usually to take eleven people on a trip to Mombasa would have been very expensive, but we got to hire a kombi—a twelve seater van, with our own personal driver, to take us to the hotel and for excursions into the city of Mombasa.

On our way down to Mombasa, the gas filter got clogged and we had to hang out in the city of Machakos, forty-five minutes outside of Nairobi, to wait for a new filter to be delivered. Knowing it would take a couple of hours, because the part was coming from Nairobi, we went our separate ways to look around the city. Being pregnant, I was hungry whenever I wasn't nauseous. So I told Daryl I was going to take the kids and get something to eat. He, my parents and several others said they would come, too.(When we first formed out team, Machakos was one of the areas we thought about working in.)

Finding a place that looked pretty clean, with tables and chairs and menus, we sat down. Looking over the items available we explained what some of the wording meant to the group. We told them that almost everything came with 'chips' or French fries. Also, that the most dependable food item (in that it looked and tasted like you expected it to) was an omelet. Omelets were generally offered 'western style' or with cheese. 'Western-style' in Kenya meant it was prepared with chopped tomatoes, onions, mushrooms and bell peppers. When the waiter came by, I asked him if I could have a combination of the two omelets. When he said I could, I went on to tell him I would like to have the omelet with mushrooms, onions and cheese, no bell pepper or tomatoes. Also that I would like the omelet and the accompanying bacon cooked dry and didn't want any sausage at all. (Being pregnant, I got heartburn and nauseous easily and didn't want to have either on the trip.)

"Good grief, Laurie," my mother said with a hint of annoyance, "why didn't you just get something simple?"

"Toast and milk," she said to the waiter, as she handed him the menu. Everyone else ordered either western-style or cheese omelets which came with sausage, bacon and fries.

In a bit, the waiter returned with our food. Mine was prepared exactly as I had asked for it. My mother was given a glass of milk and two slices of plain bread with butter on the side. As she reached for the milk, she found that it was hot. After she told us this, we flagged down the waiter.

"I want the milk cold and the bread hot," she explained to him. As he took the food away, we all dug into the omelets we had ordered. A short while later the waiter returned. This time, when he set down the bread, there were some visible toasted lines on it, but the milk was still warm.

"Cold," my mom emphasized, touching the glass. "I want the milk cold." So, the waiter picked it up and took it away. Returning for the third time, he set down the glass of milk. When it was still warm, my mother sighed and said, "That's okay."

The rest of our group was just about finished with our hearty breakfasts by that time. We had to laugh when she said, "I was trying to order the simplest thing. Who would have thought it would have caused so much trouble?"

Finally, the *kombi* was repaired. The driver, trying to make up for lost time, drove over the potholed tarmac with gusto. Halfway through the trip we asked him to stop at a hotel so we could use a clean bathroom. Also, those that hadn't eaten the big breakfast with us were now hungry and wanted to find something to eat. There were only a couple of bathrooms for public use, so it took a while for all of us to use the facilities. But the important thing was that they were clean, had toilet paper, they all flushed and had sinks where we could wash our hands!

While we were waiting for the others to finish, my mom asked if we could get the driver to slow down. I had placed her near the front of the van so she could get a good view of the countryside, which she likes to look at as she travels. When we took our seats this time, I moved her towards the back. She said she liked not being able to see the road and oncoming traffic because his driving was making her nervous. Daryl also started calling out, "*Pole, pole*-slow down" to the driver when he started driving too fast. (This is Swahili and sounds like po-lee, po-lee.) For the rest of the trip, different people would call out, "Pole, pole" whenever they wanted him to slow down.

What a refreshing sight the hotel was when we finally got there! After getting everyone's room assignment and making sure everyone was satisfied with their rooms, we agreed to meet again at dinner. As usual, we all had a great relaxing time while in Mombasa. One of the days, the ladies of the group wanted an excursion into town. The guys opted to stay at the hotel to relax or to swim and snorkel. The two teenage girls in our group had seen the sign for the Hard Rock Café as we drove through Mombasa on the way down and wanted to go there. The rest just wanted to 'see the sights' and look for souvenirs.

Fifty shilling note depicting Mombasa Town

We returned to the hotel in time to show off the goodies we had found, to share how we had spent our day and to find out how the other half had spent theirs. My mom was surprised to find out that my Dad, instead of resting in the room like she thought he would, had spent most of the day in the ocean playing in the waves instead. The beautiful, clear, aqua waters off the coast of East Africa is the Indian Ocean. The currents that drive the waves to the beach are warm. (It has spoilt me to any other beaches or ocean waters.) Because the water was so pleasant and enjoyable, my dad said he frolicked in the waves until the glare of the water began to give him a headache. Knowing that if he didn't take some medicine, the minor headache could turn into a migraine, he got out of the waves and returned to the hotel.

As he got to the lobby a monkey ran by with something shiny in its hand. My dad watched as the monkey climbed up into the high rafters of the vaulted ceiling in the foyer and then paused for a moment to look at its shiny new toy. Looking about my dad saw there was no one at the desk to report the incident to. Thinking the monkey had taken someone's watch or room key, he yelled up at the monkey hoping this would make him drop his shiny prize. It worked.

Startled, the monkey dropped the object so it could use both hands to climb more quickly and get out of there. After watching the monkey scamper away, my dad bent down to pick up what the monkey had dropped. It wasn't a room key or a watch as he thought, but a small metal box with French writing on it. Having lived in the Cajun French area of southern Louisiana for twenty-five years, my dad had picked up a bit of French. Flipping it over, he read the words *'medicament pour mal de tète'*—medicine for a bad head or headache medicine.

"After I got to the room, I took one of the tablets and lay down. My headache was better after a few minutes." He said, concluding how he had spent his day.

"Teddie (my dad's nickname), I don't believe you. I think you're just telling a story!" my mother told him. My dad, known for his storytelling ability, both real and fiction, laughed as he opened up the nightstand and handed her the little metal box.

"Well, I'll say!" my mother said. (He still has that little box. It's lying on a shelf with other little mementos my dad has kept over the years.)

Having visitors not only gave us a break from our daily activities, but also gave us a chance to visit and catch up on what had been going on in each others lives—be they family, friends, co-workers or people from church. Every (American) summer we had guests, interns from colleges or friends of a friend, passing through or looking to spend the night or a few days or weeks with us. Being that it was the American summer-time, but the Kenyan wintertime, people were surprised when we told them to be sure and bring a jacket. Because of movies, people seem to think of Africa as always being unbearably hot.

Lydia on another Mombasa vacation, Notice the wooden hand carved dhow to the left

Having so many people come in the 'summer' made those months in our life hectic at times. Visits from people not during those times, seemed more special because we could relax more and not be pulled in so many directions. Daryl's parents came at a time like that, in the month of October. They came to us from India where they had just spent about five weeks doing mission work there. Since their time with us was short, they probably would have been content just being with their first grand-daughter, Lydia, who was nine months old at the time. But like always, we crammed as much as we could into the time we had with them. The trip over to Kenya was so long and expensive we wanted to give whoever came our way exposure to as many different things as possible.

Carl and Louise Cole, an elder and his wife from our overseeing congregation in Muskogee, OK came in February when Lydia was only three weeks old. The church had thrown her a baby shower before they came to see us. When we picked them up from the airport, we were surprised to see how much luggage they had for just the two of them. As it turned out, their carry-on pieces were all they had brought for themselves. The four large suitcases were for us and held a computer and printer (laptops were not available at that time), a travel port-a-crib, diapers—both cloth and disposable and enough clothes to last Lydia, for the two years before we went to America on our first furlough. I never had another little girl to wear all those clothes, but there were many little girls, American and Kenyan alike who got the use of those clothes for years!

It was always fun to see what parts of Kenya visitors found interesting, difficult, encouraging or scary. We could usually figure this out by the places they wanted us to stop so they could take a picture. The majority of pictures in this book came from photos our families took when they came to visit us. I'm so thankful they did so we could have a record of our time in Kenya. To us, our life had become 'normal' and we hardly gave pictures a thought except to document the kids' birthdays.

Lesson Learned

Don't look a gift horse (or monkey) in the mouth.
Be thankful for God's provisions especially
if it's in a form that takes you by surprise.

Standing on the Equator at the town of Nanyuki, Lydia
was 4 1/2, Steven was 2 1/2 and I was pregnant with Lee

(Note: My hair is extremely short because the person
cutting my hair didn't know English very well. I said to
<u>cut off</u> an inch and she thought I said to <u>cut it</u> an inch!)

SIXTEEN

ƚaman ak lo

(tah mahn ak lo)

"An eye for an eye and a tooth for a tooth!"

"Very good. That way the whole world will be blind and toothless."
Movie: Fiddler on the Roof

TRIBAL CLASHING

For the most part, Kenya was a peaceful place to live. Yes, in the big cities there were muggings, where cars and other items got stolen. But with hand guns being illegal and the jail system being primitive, the volume and types of crimes were not the same as in the U.S. By using common sense, locking up valuables, staying in well-lit places with lots of people after dark, you were pretty much safe wherever you went. I really felt no fear; during the years we lived in Sotik. As a safety precaution, we had an understanding on our team that the women would be home no later than thirty minutes after dark when we went away from home without the men. If we weren't home by then, the guys would come looking for us. On the other hand, if the men didn't come home until 10 p.m. or maybe not at all, the other men on the team didn't necessarily go out looking for them. It depended on where they went, if it had rained (and they were delayed from mud), if they were all alone, etc.

Daryl told me he didn't want me to send someone out to look for him, no matter what. He said if he ever got stuck in a muddy road so badly that he couldn't get out, he would either sleep in the car or walk over to someone's house and ask to be put up for the night. The Kipsigis were very hospitable people so if he did this, it wouldn't have caused a problem. Even so, it didn't keep us ladies from occasionally fretting, worrying and praying until our guys got home some nights.

Kenyan hospitality, hands are washed and then meals are eaten by hand from shared bowls (my dad seated by Daryl)

One time, Kathy Rogers and I were out together at a ladies meeting some distance from our houses. We had just dropped off the last of our passengers from that area and were heading back home, pleased because we were ahead of schedule. Then we heard the telltale thump, thump, thump, which could only mean a flat tire. We pulled over hoping against hope that it was something else, but it was not.

"I haven't changed a tire on one of these trucks before. Have you?" Kathy asked.

"No, but surely between the two of us, we can figure it out." I replied.

With the help of the book from the glove compartment, we figured out how to lower the spare to the ground from underneath the truck bed where it was stored. Together we dragged it out and rolled it over to the tire that was flat. As we stood there trying to figure out where to put the jack in order to lift the truck; a man approached asking us if he could be of assistance. We looked at each other for guidance and then gave a shrug as in, *Why not?* (I for one had experienced this same scenario many times when traveling with Daryl when we would get a flat. I'm sure Kathy had, too. People were always quick to offer assistance. Either for the few shillings we would give them for helping us out or simply to be 'neighborly'.)

He definitely knew what he was doing and made quick work out of changing the tire. We were happy when we realized we wouldn't be late after all. When he lowered the truck all the way down, we found out the spare was also flat. *"Oh no, what are we going to do now?"* I thought. By now, a crowd had gathered. Everyone was giving us suggestions in a blend of Kipsigis, English and Kiswahili which only made the situation worse. After about ten minutes of that, a *matatu* pulled up, packed full of people. The driver stopped and asked (in halting English) if we needed help.

I don't think very fast on my feet, but Kathy who had been a nurse before coming to Kenya, could. She asked if he would be willing to take a note to our houses in Sotik after he dropped off his passengers. When he said he would, Kathy quickly scribbled off a note telling her husband, Eddie, approximately where we were.

She then told the driver, "Ask anyone in town where the *wazungu* live and they will tell you where our houses are."

After he left, we shook everyone's hands thanking them for their help and gave the man who changed the spare a few shillings. Now that it was beginning to get dark, we climbed inside the truck and locked the doors to wait. For the most part, the crowd dispersed. Some children lingered and stared. Others passed by and called out, "How are you?"

Kathy and I tried to just ignore it all and talked about this and that until there was a knock on the window. The windows had fogged up during our conversation. Rolling the window down to see better, we saw a young man standing there with a flashlight. Talking to us in very good English, he told us the village knew of our trouble and he would like to offer us his home to wait in. Asking for a moment to discuss it, we rolled the window back up so we could talk it over privately. By our calculations, we had at least an hour to wait. With the sun having gone down, it had become chilly. Since he said he was speaking for the village, we figured he didn't mean us any harm. Dashing off another note for the guys, just in case they got to the truck before we returned, we got out of the truck and locked it up. Sticking close together, we followed where he led.

Up ahead we saw a well-lit house, not a hut. Here, seemingly in the middle of nowhere, was a nice brick house with electricity. Going inside, we saw that it was furnished with store bought tables, chairs and a sofa. It looked very similar to our own homes. Directing us to the sofa where we were to wait, I noticed the coffee table in front of it had doilies on top and magazines and newspapers on the shelf underneath it. When the man left the room, Kathy and I turned to each other and smiled. Relieved, we sat back and begin to relax.

A short time later, a woman walked into the room carrying a tray. Sitting this down on the table, she greeted us with the typical handshake and then asked if we would like to have some tea. After saying yes, I looked down at the tray and was astonished to see a china tea pot with china cups and saucers. Pouring us each a cup of tea and handing them to us, she then left the room. Our eyes followed her in disbelief. It all seemed so surreal. I felt like I was in a Kenyan version of *The Twilight Zone!*

While we sipped our tea, the man came back into the room. We told him who we were and he in turn told us a little about himself. He was attending Kenyatta University in Nairobi and had come home for a visit. After we visited for a while longer, Kathy told him she thought our husbands would be arriving soon and that we should be at the truck when they got there. If we were not there when they arrived, they may be worried, she clarified. He nodded to show he understood.

Leaving the room, he came back with the lady who had brought us the tea tray. Thanking her and telling her goodbye, we again followed him out into the darkness. Getting back to the truck, we thanked him for all he had done and told him we would be fine to wait by ourselves. He didn't need to wait with us. Climbing inside the truck, we locked the doors as he turned and slipped back into the dark of the night. In about fifteen minutes, our husbands showed up. While they were changing the tire, we explained everything that had occurred and that instead of sitting out in the cold; we had spent the evening in the lap of luxury, seemingly in the middle of nowhere. Surprisingly, within a couple of years, this feeling of security would be sorely tested by tribal clashing in our area.

Antony came to our house to discuss an upcoming appointment. Instead of discussing that, we talked about other events that were occurring in our vicinity. He told us that everyone was talking about a Kipsigis man who had stolen some cattle from a Kisii man in retaliation for some offense. (The Kipsigis tribe and the Kisii tribe share a boundary line and are enemies.) When the Kisii man came to take back his stolen cattle, he in turn retaliated by hitting the Kipsigis man in the leg with a *panga*—machete. The Kipsigis man's leg became so infected that he died. Now the fight was growing larger and larger affecting more people than just the two original families.

Antony and Joseph were from the same village of Chebongi, near Sotik, where the fighting had broken out. Kipsang lived in another village, a thirty minute walk in the opposite direction, but they were all aware of what was going on. Antony said we may not be able to have a meeting that week due to the turmoil. We found this hard to believe in such a quiet part of the country. On the day of the appointment we loaded up the car as usual and drove into the village to collect Antony. As we drove deeper into the remote countryside, we noticed that things seem to be quieter than usual. There was hardly anybody walking alongside the road. It didn't really strike me as to how subdued it was until we reached our destination and no kids came running out to wave and shout the customary question, "How are you?!"

Getting out of the car, we walked onto the compound and still we saw no one. Finally, as we got to the front door, the owner came out to greet us. We went inside the house to wait for more people to come to the meeting, but no one came. We were served tea and told we probably should have no more meetings for a while. The drive back was just as eerily somber and devoid of people. When we got home that night, Daryl went over to see Eddie while I fixed supper. (This was just a couple of weeks after I rolled the Range Rover. The vehicle was being assessed for damages in Nairobi. We were using the Vick's truck while they were on furlough.)

Daryl came back saying Eddie had a similar experience when he went out that day. They had talked it over and agreed that we should just stay home for the rest of the week as a precaution, like both of our language helpers/co-church planters had suggested. I thought it was all 'much ado about nothing', until one night a house just simply disappeared.

One morning, Kathy came to the house to ask, "Did you hear any kind of noises last night?"

"No. Why do you ask?" I responded.

"The house on the corner…it's gone." She said.

"What do you mean, 'it's gone'?" I asked.

"It's just not there anymore. A Kisii woman was living there. Now she and the house are gone." She explained.

Since it was just around the corner from our houses, I walked down there to see what she was talking about. That house was not just your typical African clapboard shack or mud hut. It was a house built of brick and mortar, with a *mabati*— corrugated iron roof, and windows and doors. Granted, the water was supplied to the house by a simple spigot outside in the yard, not plumbed into the house. And the windows didn't have glass in them, but it was a more 'permanent' dwelling than many of the huts a short distance away.

I stood there looking at the knocked down barbed wire fence in disbelief. The night before when we went to bed, there had been a house standing there. Now, the water spigot, the wooden stand used to air-dry dishes and a few bricks, scattered here and there, were all that remained of the dwelling. How could it just disappear? How could this type of destruction be carried out with no one hearing a thing? I didn't even remember hearing a dog bark. No longer feeling it was 'much ado about nothing', I returned home to wait for Daryl to return with Antony. They got back earlier than usual because the meeting, even further away from Sotik, was also postponed to another time, because of the tribal clashing. The severity of the situation was finally beginning to sink in.

Daryl asked Antony, "Are we in danger? Should we leave until this is over?"

Antony responded, "This fighting is between the Kipsigis and the Kisii. No one will bother you. They know you are here to teach people about God." Relief flooded over me until he continued with, "Unless someone runs in here to seek sanctuary. Whoever is after him won't care who you are. They will burn down the house to get him, if they have to."

Registration document required by the Kenyan government

After getting Lydia three years old, and Steven one year old, to sleep, I was deep in thought as I got myself ready for bed. Daryl cut off the lights just before coming to bed. On the way there, he paused at the bedroom window to look outside because something had caught his attention.

He said, "There's a hut burning over there," pointing out the bedroom window to the hill across the valley from us. Before I could get out of bed to take a look for myself, he said, "There's another one!"

Looking out our window at the fires in the valley, another thatched roof began burning, so I asked, "What should we do?"

"There's nothing we can do. I'll make sure all the doors and windows are locked," he said, and then left to do that.

It took me a while to settle down and go to sleep, but I eventually did. A few hours later, a little after midnight, I was awakened by the sound of running feet and ulalelling—the universal African cry of alarm and despair. (This sound is made by rapidly moving the tongue on the roof of you mouth as you make a high pitched cry.)

Wide awake now, I got out of bed, shook Daryl awake and said, "People are running down the hillside by the house!"

Getting out of bed, he looked out the window and then listened for a bit. "They're running past the house down to the river. They're not interested in us." Then he turned and went back to bed.

"You're going back to bed?!" I exclaimed. "There's no way I can go to sleep, now. I think I'll pack a bag; just in case we have to leave quickly and then I'll be able to sleep."

"Okay," he said with a yawn, already half sleep.

Throwing on clothes, I grabbed a small suitcase from the top of the closet. In this, I put in a complete change of clothes for Daryl and me. Going to Lydia's room, I gently pulled a dress down over her pajamas and put socks and shoes on her feet. Grabbing a couple of outfits, toys and books, I took them to our room and put them in the suitcase. Going to Steven's room, I put his shoes on over his sleeper feet, grabbed diapers and pins, a couple of outfits and a few toys to pack for him.

Feeling a bit better, I turned my thoughts toward food. I went into the kitchen and grabbed my woven shopping bag to see what I had on hand that we could take with us. In it I put a couple of cartons of UHT—milk that needed no refrigeration, a box of crackers, a can of tuna, fruit, chocolate bars and other things like that which needed no refrigeration or were easy to eat. Passing by the bathroom on the way to our bedroom, I stopped to grab our small first-aid kit and a roll of toilet paper. Getting my purse and Daryl's wallet from the night-stand, I put those in the suitcase, too. Then I threw in a bar of soap, a couple of towels and *kangas*. (*Kangas* are used for all kinds of things, including carrying children on your back. I thought these might come in handy if we had to abandon the car and walk with the kids.) I finally sat down to think some more and rest. Unable to think of anything else to pack, I stretched out, fully clothed, shoes and all, on top of the bed. After a bit, I took off my shoes, set them beside the bed and finally went to sleep.

The next morning I felt a little silly when I saw the packed bags and the kids asleep with their shoes on. I gently removed their shoes so I wouldn't wake them. Leaving everything else packed to deal with later; I took the food with me when I went into the kitchen to make breakfast. Later that morning; my curiosity got the better of me and I went down to see if Kathy and Eddie had heard anything.

"Did you hear that commotion last night?" I asked.

"I sure did!" She said. "I got up and packed a bag."

"Me, too!" I said, in surprise.

"What did you pack?" she asked.

As I told her about the items she would say "Me, too" or "I hadn't thought of that."

Then we went over what she had packed. Many of our items were the same, but these were some of the items she had included that I hadn't thought of: a jerry can of filtered water, their passports, family pictures, a map of Maasai Mara Game Park, flashlights, matches and a can opener.

"Why did you pack a map of Maasai Mara?" I asked, thinking that was surely put in there by mistake.

"It's a way to cross the border into Tanzania if the main roads are closed and we need to get out of the country," she explained, showing the route they had highlighted on the map.

"Get out of the country?" I asked, blankly.

"Yeah, we might need to find a way out of Kenya if the fighting gets really bad," she explained.

We parted ways and added to our suitcases with the ideas we got from each other. After some long, tense weeks, the dispute was settled and things got back to normal. As it turned out, those suitcases were never needed. But it made me realize how quickly things could change here. Since we were going home on a furlough shortly anyway, I decided to pack up some things and return them to America because they were too special to me to take the chance of losing them.

After I got the trunk home, I asked my mom if I could store it in their attic until we returned from Kenya. She said I could if I showed her what was in it. Opening the trunk, I began pulling out the items to show them to her. Many of the things were what you would expect to find: our wedding album, pictures of the kids, baby clothes and shoes, a couple of handmade quilts, my high school and college yearbooks. But something that surprised my mom was when I pulled out a couple of cloth 'rag' dolls. One of them I got from my sister, Carla, when I was a young girl. It was a girl with yellow yarn for hair and a long antebellum dress. My sister, Teddie, received one just like it, but with brown 'hair'.

The other cloth doll was one of a set my sister Teddie and I got for Christmas one year. Teddie and I are only a year and a half apart. So, we played together most of the time and shared a lot of our things. The doll set my mom made for us was a boy and a girl doll with brown yarn hair. She had covered a fruit basket to make it look like a bassinet, complete with a little pillow and a quilted blanket. She had also made them each a little pair of pajamas to wear to bed.

We loved that set and played with them all the time. Even after I left the girl doll outside one night and the dog chewed off half of one of her braids, she didn't loose her appeal. The dampness from the dew eventually left some tiny spots of mold. I just thought of them as grey freckles, since I had freckles, too.

When my mom saw that doll, she picked it up and fingered the braid that was half chewed off and quietly said, "I had *no idea* you cared so much about this doll. That Christmas was a really hard one for us, we had no money. I made those dolls with stuff from the rag bag."

"You did?" I said. "Well I never knew it! You even made them a little bed and some pajamas."

"Oh yeah, I'd forgotten about that," she replied. Giving me a hug, she said, "Well, I'm glad that it meant so much to you. I had no idea."

"Well, it means even more to me now," I replied, returning the hug.

But my mom didn't keep those dolls in the attic. Whenever I went home on furlough she would have the two cloth dolls displayed in some way. Once, they were lying amongst the pillows on the bed in the guestroom. Another time, they lay side-by-side in a little antique baby doll bed. And the last time, they were with a dog and Howdy Doody doll my older brother, Steve, had when he was a child. I'm glad I put those dolls in that trunk or we never would have made those special memories between the two of us.

LESSON LEARNED

You never know what things have made a special memory for someone else. So, treat people's possessions as if everything is of importance.

Not a good picture of Daryl, but it shows the hills behind him where we could see the huts burning

Fence beside our house that the people were running past.
Barely visible between Daryl and posts, are the tiny trees we
had planted that eventually become a big, tall, thick hedge

SEVENTEEN
taman ak tisab
(tah mahn ahk tis ahb)

"I don't want to live someone else's idea of how to live.
Don't ask me to do that. I don't want to find out
one day that I'm at the end of someone else's life."
Movie: Out of Africa

TRYING
SOMETHING DIFFERENT

Having to work hard for all the meals that we ate gave us a deeper appreciation of them. Most of the meals eaten in the village were tied to the very land upon which we sat, consuming them. The *kimiyet*—corn meal mixture, *sakuma wiki*—kale-like greens, beans, potatoes, and *chaik* were the basic components of the diet of the Kipsigis people and was usually grown by their efforts or sold to purchase items they didn't have. Our gardens had a different variety of items in them than could be found locally. We grew foods like lettuce, broccoli, bell peppers, okra and hot peppers to name a few. By doing that it augmented the local fare and helped give us the variety we were more accustomed to.

The big market day was Sunday. Just about every Sunday morning before going off to church I would grab my woven shopping basket and drive out to the field set aside for the open air market. Since most of the food was the same, I chose food based on the person selling it. I gravitated towards the older woman whose clothes didn't look as nice or the woman with a couple of kids, people who seemed to need the income more. Regardless of what was being sold, the routine was the same. You walked the pathway between the brightly colored *kangas* or burlap bags. These were used to carry their items to market and then as a way to define their selling area and to display their wares. As you walked by, the ladies would call out the price hoping to catch your attention. The price was only a starting point and started out much higher than it ordinarily would be. Once you stopped to look at their food, the bargaining began. The only set prices anywhere were in the grocery stores. Everywhere else you went, you were expected to 'bar—gain.'

At first it was overwhelming because I didn't know the languages they were speaking. Sotik, being situated on the border of two tribal groups and on one of the main roads, attracted a variety of people on market day. Typically, the languages heard were Kipsigis, Kisii, Kiswahili and English. Daryl went with me until I learned enough Kipsigis to be able to negotiate prices on my own. On market day, the fruits and vegetables were at their peak and at the best prices. You could still get fruits and vegetables from a stall closer to the road throughout the week, but the prices were higher and the produce tended to be a bit shriveled and spotty. So it was always better to go Sunday morning. Haltingly at first, and gradually with more confidence, I learned to bargain. The best 'deals' I got were whenever one of the kids came with me. When the kids wanted to come with me, I would buy a section of finger bananas first thing and then they would contentedly stand by my side munching away while I shopped.

One year for Christmas, Beverly Bell, one of our missionary friends in Kisumu, had tiny little woven baskets made for her baked goods. When I saw these, I asked her if she had a spare I could buy for Lydia, who loved all manner of purses. Whenever I went to the market after that, Lydia liked to go too and bring her little basket. The ladies got a laugh whenever they saw her. Without fail, they gave a chuckle, calling to their neighbor to look at the tiny bag. After giving me the produce I had purchased, they would say '*agobo lakwet*—for the child' as they dropped an extra one into her bag. I would then try to get her to say '*kongoi*—thank you' (Kalenjin) or '*asante*' (Kiswahili). Sometimes she would act shy and not do it. But, if she did, they would give another chuckle in delight and tell their neighbor about that, too.

Steven 'driving' a tractor in a t-shirt and diaper

Steven was more of a ham and liked to make people laugh, from an early age. He was my big eater, too. Steven learned Kipsigis phrases before he was two because it meant getting wider access to food. On one occasion our workers were having their tea break out on the breezeway.

When Steven saw them drinking chaik he said to me, "I want some chaik."

Getting a cup out of the cupboard for him, I was struck by an inspiration and said, "Steven, take this cup to Kipsang and say *Amache chaik.*"

"No, I can't say it," he said sulkily. "You say it."

"No. If you want chaik, you need to ask Kipsang for it yourself." Seeing his hesitation, I said, "Say—ah," breaking the phrase into smaller segments and coaxing him phonetically.

"Ah" he repeated halfheartedly.

"Mah-chay" I continued.

"Mah-chay" he repeated, with a bit more effort.

"*Chaik!*" I said with enthusiasm, because I knew he knew that word already.

"*Chaik!*" he repeated back, with equal enthusiasm.

"*Amache chaik!*" I said, putting the phrase together.

"*Amache chaik,*" he repeated, grinning.

"*Amache chaik,*" I repeated, handing him the cup and motioning for him to go outside, after he said it again.

Steven walked outside and sat near Kipsang holding the cup on his lap, cradled in his hands. Kipsang and Joseph knew what he wanted because the kids would often join them when they were having chaik. As Kipsang started to take the cup from Steven, I got his attention and shook my head no. He gave me a puzzled look but obliged and went back to sipping his tea.

I stepped back out of the doorway and moved to the dining room window where I could see and hear what was going on without being so visible. Kipsang and Joseph quietly went back to a more subdued conversation while Steven sat there with his head down. No more than a minute later, Steven looked up and over at me. I gave him a nod and motioned with a wave of my hand to encourage him to go ahead and try. Looking back at the guys, Steven blurted out, "*Amache chaik!*"

They laughed and nodded, finally understanding what had been going on. I carried out another cup to Kipsang so he could pour the chaik back and forth between the two cups in an attempt to cool it down from the scalding temperature they preferred, to a more tolerable temperature for a toddler. As Kipsang continued transferring the chaik from one cup to another, he would slowly say, "*Amache chaik.*"

Steven sat there swinging his legs, with a big dimpled grin that went from ear to ear, very pleased with himself and said, "*Amache chaik,*" again; this time with great enthusiasm.

They all settled down again and in a relaxed fashion, drank their chaik. Periodically over the next fifteen minutes or so of their tea break, Steven would say "*Amache chaik*" whenever there was a lull in the conversation because he continued to get a laugh or a smile when he said it.

From that point on, Steven had an 'in'. Usually when we went to a village, he and Lydia would scamper off to be with the other kids; after a bit, they would come back to sit near us. If they took longer that normal to return, I would go look for them. More often than not I had to look no further than the cooking hut. Going inside, I would see Steven sitting there with a cup in one hand, something to eat in the other and a big grin on his face.

The mama near the fire would say, "*Imwae imache chaik*—He said he wanted some chaik."

Lydia, who would rather play than eat, would usually be out running around with the other kids. Situations out in the village, or out and about Kenya, were not always so ideal. With our kids being so fair and blue-eyed, people were drawn to them, wherever we went. You didn't see many white kids out in the villages unless they were missionary kids.

Most times they were treated well, like the occasion we were travelling in the Amboseli National (Game) Park with some summer interns. We had to pull over and stop because the Maasai were driving their cattle and goats to a well that had been dug for the community in this drought prone region. Using the opportunity to stretch, we put Lydia, about a year and a half old, into the bed of the truck where she could run around safely away from the herd that was surrounding us. Catching sight of the *wazungu*, the Maasai strolled over to get a better look at us.

(The Maasai tribe is one of the most authentic ethnic tribes of Kenya and Tanzania. They are a semi-nomadic people that are allowed to freely criss-cross the borders of these two countries. Despite education and western influences, they have clung to their traditional way of life.)

The interns were thrilled for the opportunity to see the famous Maasai. Much to my surprise these fierce looking men, holding spears, wrapped in blankets, with their hair braided and lacquered with red ochre were just as curious about us as we were about them. They exchanged cameras for spears so each could take a look at the details of the other. When I walked up to them holding Lydia, they reached out to touch her white cheeks and feel her fine strawberry-blond hair, with big grins on their faces. That was a sight I won't soon forget. Dust in the air, cattle lowing waiting their turn at the well and the Maasai holding my little girl, quite a dissimilarity.

Sometimes the contrast in culture didn't work so well. There were times the kids would come to me crying because they had been pinched or their hair pulled. We knew it was just natural curiosity and not meanness on the Kenyans part but it was hard to explain that to a child. Even not being a child, there were times when being in the village was just too much for us to take, too. This occurrence seemed to be happening more frequently for all of us. Taking over someone else's work is both a blessing and a curse. We didn't have to go through the

'birth pains' of breaking new ground. However, we had to deal
with the awkwardness of the 'teenage years' without the prior
relationship the former team had spent years building. At times
it was a struggle to go out day after day, trying to make yourself
fit into a mold that was not of your choosing.

Summer interns, Lydia and some Maasai

We began to find other things to do outside of our
activities with the Kenyans in hopes of helping this strain. I
joined the EAWL, East African Women's League, a charitable
organization primarily made up of British expatriates who ran
the tea estates around the country. It was one of the highlights
of the month to attend an organizational meeting. Janet Allison
was a member of long-standing and brought us all to our first
meeting. Kathy didn't care for it, but Brenda and I enjoyed
them. We would get 'dolled up' for the occasion by wearing
nice dresses, high-heeled shoes, jewelry, perfume, make-up and
style our hair in something other than a ponytail.

At the meeting, we would have a guest speaker who spoke on a variety of subjects. Or we discussed how to raise money for the local deaf school that we supported with our fundraisers. After the meeting, we would have 'high tea', sit around and chat. That was the part that we truly went for and liked the best. They found us quaint because we were learning the tribal language of the Kipsigis, instead of the nationally spoken Kiswahili many of them had learned. They couldn't believe that we actually went inside the huts in the villages and ate their food with them.

Through this monthly interaction we became friends and they opened up their homes and estates to us. Each tea estate had some sort of sports facility built on them to ensure that they could keep themselves physically fit, in those remote pockets of the world. One estate had tennis courts and another had a hedge enclosed private pool, complete with dressing rooms and a snooker/pool table. A different one had squash courts that we tried to play racquetball in. And they all had plant nurseries where they grew produce and flowers for the 'garden', not the yard like we called it.

Daryl would often play a set of tennis with Malcolm and Liz Johnston on our day off, while I walked their lovely 'English' garden with the children. Their house worker would bring out finger sandwiches, tea and cake as refreshments. We ate those properly out on the lawn, sitting in chairs, with the table covered in linen and a china tea service.

On one occasion, Liz put milk in my tea when I had asked to take it without it. Taking the teacup from me, she just flung the contents to the ground. Surprised, I said, "Liz, you didn't have to throw it out. I could have drunk it like that."

She responded with a smile, "Don't worry, we have plenty of tea!"

We couldn't help but laugh when she said that. We were after all, sitting on the grounds of a tea estate, whose factory exported its tea all over the world. And not only that; but we were surrounded in all directions, as far as the eye could see, by acres and acres of rolling tea fields. Indeed, they did have plenty of tea and some of the best I've ever tasted!

One month when Brenda and I had the league ladies meet at our houses, we realized we had a fondness for each other's magazines. They were as fascinated by America as we were with England. After looking at our American decorations and then eating our American food, they asked us to do a demonstration for one of the upcoming meetings. Flattered, we agreed. Brenda and I brainstormed and came up with a couple of ideas each.

I took down the balloon shade from the bath-room, because it was small, easy to carry and to pass around for a demonstration. Then I drew up the instructions on how to make it showing how to figure the proper yardage, or meters, so fabric could be purchased locally to make the curtains. I also brought a homemade decorated vine wreath and told them what vines could be used to make it. Brenda, who is a good cook, made some American desserts showing what she substituted for certain ingredients in Kenya. She also showed them how to design, cut out and paint with your own stencils using products from Kenya. We were a hit! They thought of us as being very adaptable to our environment; we thought of them as a little oasis of civility.

While we ladies had the East African Women's League, as a distraction of sorts, the men had golf. All of our husbands joined the Kericho Golf Club, playing solo or all together whenever they could manage it. This was Daryl's 'little oasis of civility.' It was supposed to be a way for him to blow off steam, but it didn't always work out that way. With the Kericho Club being in such a rural setting, he occasionally had to wait for a cow to be chased off the green so he could finish the hole. Once he even had a monkey snatch up his golf ball and scamper up a tree with it. Like I said, it wasn't always conducive to relieving stress.

Another thing that helped with the strain I felt at times by living in such a rural setting was a great friendship that developed between our family and a British family that moved into town. At different times throughout that first term, everyone on our team became disenchanted with Kenya. Everyone that was, but me. I just couldn't understand what the big deal was and why they were having such a hard time with Kenya. I loved everything about it! (Those feelings are often referred to as the 'honeymoon period' in missions.)

When we come back after our first furlough, culture shock hit me right between the eyes! Everything seemed so dirty, so crude, so slow, so—I didn't know what! But what I did know for sure was that I wanted out of there!! It didn't help matters that I became pregnant shortly after returning and that I was nauseous most of the pregnancy. I even had to quit going out in the village with Daryl because the washboard dirt roads started making me cramp. I was so thankful when the time came to leave Sotik to go into Nairobi to give birth to Steven.

On our way out of town, we went a different route. We were surprised to see two pre-fabricated houses going up in a field on the outskirts of town. We speculated on who the houses could possibly be for. Jokingly, at one point, I said, "Maybe it's someone who has a little girl that Lydia can play with!"

Lydia had Josiah Vick as a playmate. They were great friends and had many hours and days that they spent together. But she was a girl, he was a boy and there was a two year age difference. So it was understandable that they didn't always like to play the same things. As thankful as I was that she had someone close to her age to play with, and even though they played well together, there were times that I just wanted her to have a little girl that she could play dolls, dress-up and other girly things with.

We left Sotik a week before Steven's due date, because I started having Braxton Hicks contractions almost daily. At my eight month check-up for Steven, the doctor said I looked like I could have him at any time. I felt like we were pushing it to go only a week before he was due and was worried about the possibility of having him locally. But, like most things, the worrying was pointless. He wound up being two weeks late. By the time we finally got back home and resumed our daily activities, it was almost a month since we last saw those prefabricated houses.

The addition to our house was getting its finishing touches when we came home from the hospital at that time, too. (We hoped it would be completed before we left for Nairobi so we could oversee the construction. But like many building projects, it took longer than anticipated.) In the midst of painting, moving furniture and doing other things, I had forgotten all about those other houses. Frankly, in my adjustment to being the mother of an active toddler and a newborn, I didn't have much time to spare to think about anything else.

One day, coming home earlier than he expected, Daryl decided to swing by the prefab houses to see if the new occupants had arrived. Seeing toys in the yard, he figured they must have children. So Daryl decided to stop and say hello and to see how old the kids were. He was surprised when the door opened up to a petite blonde-haired, blue-eyed lady and her children. After introductions were made, she told Daryl he should come again to bring the kids and me, so we could meet..

Arriving home minutes later, Daryl told me about them and said, "Laurie, they're British and they have three little girls! Grab the kids and let's go over there for a visit."

We did and there was an instant connection between us. Over the next year or so, we spent quite a lot of time together, in and out of each other's houses. She came with Brenda and me to the EAWL meetings. I thought it was funny when she said she was embarrassed to speak around the tea estate ladies because they spoke the 'Queen's English.' When I said their accents all sounded the same to me; she assured me there was a big difference. Having that time with Mike and Carole Fenton and their three girls, Meg, Sally and Beth was just what we ALL needed. I told her she and her family were an answer to our prayers, but she claimed I was hers. So we just agreed that God put us together. We both wound up moving away from Sotik within the year. We visited them in Nottingham, England (famous for the tales of Robin Hood), on our way back to the States on furloughs. Nowadays, we keep in touch by email.

'The Girls' on the porch swing in the breezeway

For a time after they left, our work seemed to improve because we were in good spirits. But, once again, little by little, discontentment crept back in and we had to make ourselves go out to appointments. Daryl seemed to be having a harder time of it than me because I was occupied with the children. We knew we needed to try something different if we wanted to stay in Kenya, which we did. We just didn't have a clue as to what that 'something different' was. At one of the Thanksgiving get-togethers we had in Nairobi every year, Daryl and I were approached to join a Board of Trustees for the new guest house that was being built in Karen. Karen is a suburb just outside of Nairobi, named after the Karen Coffee Company, owned by Baroness Karen von Blixen-Finecke. That area is now famous for one of the books she wrote and the movie made about her time in Kenya both named, Out of Africa. (Her home and a small portion of the original vast estate are open to the public.)

I think I was chosen for my design and decorating background. One reason Daryl was chosen was because he liked to garden and we had a beautiful yard to prove it. The guest house desperately needed both of those services to get it ready to receive guests. It was nice to feel like we had something to contribute that was wanted and valued during a time when we felt otherwise. Our team did not make us feel unappreciated; it was just the way we felt at the time. We both had grown a lot from our experiences in Sotik, but we could tell that our time there was drawing to a close. We knew we were the flexible types needed to do missions, but the fit wasn't quite right. We were glad to serve on the Board of Trustees for a time while we tried to figure out what our next step should be. Whenever we went into Nairobi to have Board Meetings for the guest house, we discussed a variety of issues, one of which was who we could get to staff, open and manage it.

As we were driving back home after one of our 'Board' trips, I asked Daryl, "What would you think about the two of us managing the guest house?"

The rest of the trip and for the next couple of months, a lot of discussion and prayer was focused on that subject. Our decision was to discuss this with the Board, our teammates and our overseeing congregation in Oklahoma to get their feedback and opinions. To our surprise, everyone was in agreement. The Sotik Team didn't want to see us go because we have been through so many things together. But, they wanted what was best for us and they knew we needed a change. The Board was glad to have someone from Kenya that understood the way things in Africa worked and also someone they all knew and trusted. Our overseeing congregation wanted to continue some sort of ministry in Kenya. They said they were happy to continue supporting us if it would be a service to others. With everyone's blessings, we began the task of pulling out of our work in Sotik; telling people goodbye and 'turning our face towards' Nairobi in preparation for our move.

Right about that same time, I started feeling nauseated on a regular basis. To be on the safe side, I went to the local hospital to take a pregnancy test. And sure enough I was unexpectedly expecting our third child. I thought the timing couldn't have been worse! We were moving into Nairobi to manage a guest house. How could I do that with a newborn, a three year old and five year old? But as always, when God has something He wants you to do, He will provide a way for you to do it. By moving to Karen to manage the guest house, called Kimbilio House (which means a place of sanctuary); He provided us with a full time cook, kitchen staff, yard workers, guards and housekeepers to keep the place spic and span! When God provides, He really provides!

With all of those people around to help us manage, Lee was well taken care of whenever I needed to leave to do something for the guest house. Lydia was able to attend a small British preschool around the corner from the house. Steven became my shopping buddy and went with me when I did the grocery shopping or other errands for the guest house. Daryl was able to teach Greek at the Great Commission School, a preacher training school in Nairobi, as well as working part-time with a new church plant. All in all, it was the right move at the right time and some of the happiest years we spent in Kenya.

LESSON LEARNED

You truly can't force a square peg into a round hole; all it gives you is frustration. You are better off using that energy on trying to figure out what you can do to change the situation.

(L to R) Steven, Lee and Lydia on the front porch of the manager's quarters at Kimbilio House

EIGHTEEN

taman ak sisit

(tah mahn   ahk   see seat)

"Do you wonder, as you watch my face;
If a wiser one, should have had my place?
But I offer all I am; for the mercy of your plan."
Song: <u>Breath Of Heaven (Mary's Song)</u> by Amy Grant

HAVING FEET IN TWO COUNTRIES

Many more things could have been written about our time in Sotik. There were lots of awkward and sometimes painful events that occurred as we were being transformed into the people God was making us into. Whatever the encounter, we were blessed (whether we realized it at the time or not). One of the things that was rather excruciating for me was learning another language. I can remember all kinds of useless facts from movies and TV shows and retain information from most of the books I've read. But dangle another language in front of me and it seems to go into a big black void, where retrieval of this information when needed is slooww. Thankfully, our children seem to have received the gift of learning languages from their father, who (to me) seems to pick them up without much effort.

Having communication be a daily struggle was a big hurdle for me to overcome. I like nothing more than to sit and have a long talk. Without being able to do so was very isolating and led to a lot of loneliness. Even being married, having children and being on a team with fellow Americans didn't always keep the loneliness at bay. I must admit that when we moved into Karen and later Nairobi, I finally felt like I was making a contribution. The big difference I think was that I could use English again to communicate. With the barrier of language taken away, I finally felt free.

We were trying so hard to do 'missions' by the same pattern as the team before us, that it became more of a burden than a guide to us both. Don't get me wrong, the previous mission 'pattern' was not being thrust upon us. Daryl and I were just so green; we felt it must be THE way to do it. Sometimes I would try to come up with something to do that was 'outside the box.' But I was either too uncomfortable to try it, couldn't figure out a way to do it, too scared to attempt it or told it wasn't wanted. I realize now I should have done them anyway. But when you feel it's all you can do just to keep your head above water, you tend to focus all your time and energy on just surviving from one day to the next.

But now looking back, I can see that God did not want me to 'DO' but to 'BE'. I feel that God had to separate me from all my comfort zones, one by one, in order for me to finally depend on Him, to just rest in Him. There are times when God wants nothing more from you than for you to "Be still and know that He is God" (Psalm 46:10 NIV). There are times He wants you to be the recipient and not the one who gives. Despite the fact that a lot of people may have felt sorry for us because we left behind our families and culture, we were given so much more because we obeyed and went when we were called. Going to Africa made us appreciative of things we never really gave a second thought to before. Things like electricity, water, food, cars, phones, hospitals and family; just to name a few. Something as simple as receiving a letter became an event.

Before Kenya, we opened each other's mail and thought nothing of it. But opening someone else's letter in Kenya felt like you were opening up their present, so we didn't do it. There were so many people that sent us cards, letters, packages and gifts that we couldn't begin to list them all, but believe me, they sustained us, blessed us and kept us connected. For one Thanksgiving to Christmas season, Duane Jenks, the minister at our church in Oklahoma, challenged the congregation to send us Christmas cards. Along with those cards, they were instructed to enclose a packet of Kool-Aid® or a packet of taco or chili seasoning mix—anything that was somewhat flat and could easily fit inside of a card.

The Jenks family had been missionaries to Brazil and knew how those simple packets would be like little treasures to us. Just like you shake or feel presents under the Christmas tree to try to figure out what's inside, we would shake, feel and *smell* those cards trying to figure out what special treat was inside of them. We were stumped by one that seemed especially lumpy and smelled of cinnamon. Opening it, we found that someone had painstakingly lined the card with sticks of Big Red® chewing gum so the card would still be relatively flat. With the mail system in Kenya being on the slow side, we enjoyed those little treasures well into February. We were all sad when they eventually stopped coming.

Everyone in our families mailed us boxes for our birthdays and for Christmas. Trying to do something nice, they would send us big packages, not realizing this was too tempting a morsel for many thieves to pass up. Every large box was opened and gone through before we ever saw it. This was done so the post office could decide how much of an import duty fee we would need to pay. When the fee was unusually high it was really just a bribe they were trying to extract from us. Whenever we received a slip of paper in our mail box in Sotik informing us that a package was waiting for us, we were both excited and a apprehensive at the same time. Since our post office was so small, we would usually have to go to another city or mail hub, hours away. It was always a little disheartening to see the opened package and wonder what we *hadn't* received. Most of what was sent found its way to us.

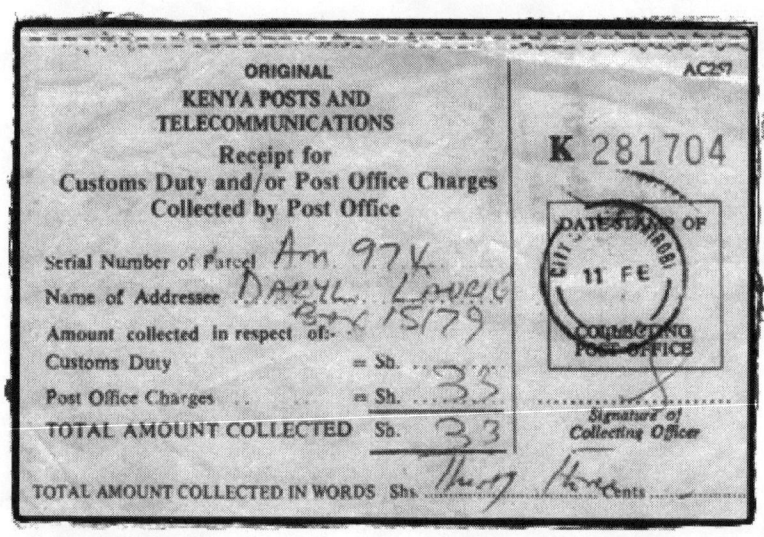

custom charges for packages sent to us from us

We tried to find ways around this by having our families mail the packages to larger cities where we had missionaries. But we didn't like the idea of putting the burden of standing in line and then paying the custom fee put on them, so after a while, we stopped doing that. After one huge package from Daryl's brother, James, took a year to get to us (even though he had paid the air fare rate), we started telling the family to just put money in our stateside bank account. My sister, Davan, was not to be deterred, though. She had me measure our post office box there in Sotik so she could mail me boxes that were small enough to fit inside that space. She had to be very creative with her gifts to find things that would fit into that 5"x 5"x 9" space, but she did. I was always amazed at how much stuff she could cram into those little boxes, but they all made it through to our post office box in Sotik. (The core of the post office was the office where purchases were made. The rest of the post office was outdoors, with a large wraparound 'porch' of cement and a deep overhanging roof to protect the boxes from the weather.)

Hearing of the hard time we were having with water, one of our supporting congregations from Memphis, TN, located at Ross Road, had their teens raise money so we could purchase a one thousand gallon water/rain tank. What a blessing that was! We were never without water again after that. Sure, we still had to be careful and re-use water and even ration it at times, but we always had it. When we later moved to Karen, water was an issue there as well, so we brought it along with us. As far as I know, it's still being of service there.

After draining it in readiness to transport it to Karen, Joseph flipped it upside-down to dry out and then we used this huge, black, plastic tank to pack into. We filled it with all manner of light-weight items to weigh it down in the lorry we had paid to carry our household goods to Karen. (There were no such things as U-Haul® moving vans.) Another reason we used the tank was because packing boxes were very hard to come by. Plastic bags like we use everywhere in the US today, were just being introduced to Kenya at that time, in 1993. So, since boxes were hard to come by, I bought a case of plastic shopping bags to pack with. One by one, those bags were filled with clothes, toys and other small items and then placed inside the tank. The kids thought it was great fun to carry a plastic bag outside in their arms, crawl through the hole in the top of the rain tank, now lying on its side, and put their bag inside of it.

They were 4 ½ and 2 ½ at the time of the move and I was five months pregnant with Lee. Instead of pulling things out of boxes, like lots of kids do at that age when you are trying to pack up to move, they were actually a big help.

Electricity rationing once a burden to us, blessed us instead by becoming a unique family time. There were actually 'brown out' times published in the newspaper so you could try to schedule your day around them. But like many things, you couldn't really depend on them to go as planned. To distract the kids from the dark, we would use those times to snuggle together and make up stories. One person would begin a story, telling it up to a certain point and then the next person would build on it, with all of us taking turns. Occasionally the lights would come back on before we were done, so we'd just cut them back off until we were finished. There's just some thing magical about telling stories by candlelight.

As stated before, food played an important part in Kenya life, but even more so during the holidays. Since we couldn't be with our families, we shared those holidays with each other. We would have to order the turkey a month or two in advance in Nairobi then make a special trip out there to pick it up. The first time it was my turn to prepare the turkey, it took me longer than I'd planned because I had to take tweezers to it and pull off some little downy feathers and quills and give it a good washing. But with these meals too, we learned to adapt and make substitutes if we didn't have the 'real' ingredients to make what we wanted. I started making carrot pie instead of pumpkin pie because the pumpkins there were yellow and didn't look as appetizing. Cashews and macadamia nuts were substituted for pecans. Chopped up Cadbury chocolate bars were used in the place of readymade 'chocolate chips'.

Even as creative as we became there just were no substitutes for some things. When fighting broke out in an area that grew and then processed the raw sugarcane into table sugar, it caused a sugar shortage in the country. (Passing through this area always made me a little homesick because I was surrounded by fields of sugarcane in the area of southern Louisiana where I grew up.)

Just when we were about to run out of sugar, we heard there was a warehouse about forty five minutes away where we could buy sugar if we purchased the whole burlap sack, costing hundreds of dollars. So, Daryl drove out there to purchase it. After bringing the sugar home, we put it in the guest room so Kipsang could divide it into the same little brown bags it was typically sold in. We paid our workers partially in sugar until the crisis was over. Those little brown bags were also given out as 'hostess gifts' whenever we went out in the village for a meeting, since people were having such a hard time finding it.

Sometimes, we had to 'think outside the box' to get some of the items we used for cooking. When we wanted large quantities of cream, we would take a container to the creamery across the valley from our houses. Once there, an employee would climb a ladder to the top of the vat carrying a large galvanized, coffee can sized ladle. He then opened up a small cover on the top, stick in the ladle and scoop out cream right off the top. Climbing back down, he'd weight it, charge us an amount then hand us the hot container of cream to take home. Dividing it up, we'd put vinegar in part to 'sour' it and sugar in the other before whisking it to make 'whipped' cream.

We got very good at adapting all sorts of American recipes to ingredients readily available in Kenya. The missionary ladies even wound up pooling those recipes into a cookbook we named "AmeriKen Cooking". I'm not very good at baking and making desserts, so it was great to have it as a guide. After having homemade pizza at someone's house in Eldoret, I thanked them for going to all the trouble to make it. They said it wasn't that difficult to make since they got the dough from the bread factory.

"What do you mean 'you got dough from the bread factory'?" I asked.

"You just go to where they make bread in your town and ask them for a loaf of raw dough or for a loaf of bread *before* it's cooked." She clarified.

Sure enough, the next time I went to Kericho, I asked around and found the bread factory I didn't even know existed. I had to go through several people before they understood that I really did want raw dough. They gave me strange looks, but sold it to me anyway. I learned this 'raw' dough was great for making cinnamon rolls, too. Having to plan so far in advance for meals, visitors and all sorts of things, really heightened the organizational skills, I hadn't even realized I possessed. It's amazing what you can achieve when you set your mind to it.

Mentioning organizational skills, makes me think about all the planning that went into furloughs. Our first furlough, just like our first Sotik 'monthly meeting' caught us unprepared. We said yes to every invitation or meal which resulted in 'furlough weight'. That is the ten to fifteen pounds missionaries typically put on when they return to America. It was also caused from eating all the 'fast food', that was not available in Kenya, as we traveled around reporting to churches, friends and families. Every time we went into a store we were like a 'kid in a candy shop' wanting everything we saw. The outcome was a buggy full of 'bargains' we just couldn't pass up. Returning to Kenya, we would be overweight, exhausted and loaded down with things that were out of place.

We lived in Kenya from 1987 to 1999. We went 'home' for about three months every two to two and a half years. As the years went by, we got better at preparing for furloughs. Once we hit the one year mark countdown to furlough, I would start compiling an indexed binder. The indexes were labeled: Flight Itinerary, Items to Pack, Things to Buy in US, Thank You Gifts, Stateside Itinerary, Contact Info and Things to Do.

The 'Flight Itinerary' tab included our flight plans, countries we would have our layovers in and things to see and do while there, if we could. Because Kenya was so far from the US, you couldn't fly there directly. We had to take two eight hour flights. One flight would be from Kenya to Europe and the other from Europe to the US. The country in Europe we would fly to would be determined by whichever airline had the cheapest airfare and/or longest layover between flights.

Lydia and Steven on a plane headed to the US, thankfully, ours kids were good travelers

Traveling with kids, we usually tried to get a room in the airport (if we didn't have an extended layover of a couple of days), so we could try to sleep before the next flight. If we couldn't sleep, we could at least rest fully stretched out on a bed. It was also nice to be able to shower and change clothes. With the door locked and outlets covered, we could let the kids safely play even if we did manage to go to sleep while resting.

Many may think that spending a day or two in Europe was a splurge that we shouldn't have taken. To us it was a way to ease back into a more modern culture. I'll never forget the first time we walked up to a glass door that automatically opened when you approached it. It startled the kids. When we walked into the lobby, there was a large bowl of bright green Granny Smith apples. When Lydia asked what they were, I realized America was just as foreign to them as the country of Belgium that we were standing in. To them, Kenya was home, not the US.

Entries under the 'Items to Pack' tab usually weren't that many. Accept for gifts, pictures and a few clothes, we didn't have that much to pack. On the return trip, our luggage would be bulging, so we brought all the suitcases we had to the States. Those suitcases would be empty for the most part, nested one inside the other, with items wedged in here and there. Very rarely did we buy clothes or shoes in Kenya. Locally made clothing was either 100% polyester or 100% cotton and neither of very good quality. Clothing of the quality we were used to in America was either imported from Europe or South Africa, making them expensive. We tried to anticipate our clothing needs for the two years in-between furloughs. We would then wear those same clothes over and over until we wore them out or grew sick of them and gave them away. American clothing, especially jeans and shoes, were popular items because they were so well made. Once Daryl did some bartering with clothes when we wanted a cupboard made. He gave Antony some clothes to make us a cupboard and Antony in turn gave some of those clothes to purchase the tree to make the cupboard with.

The 'Items to Buy in US' tab was almost the most important section of the 'furlough notebook'. That list was begun practically from the moment we returned to Kenya. You would think it would be easy to remember the much coveted items when we got to the U.S. But our mental list would get superseded by other objects we would see in the stores as we walked up and down the packed American store aisles. (We learned this the hard way our first furlough.) It was also good to keep a 'running list' on hand for those times we would get a request when someone wanted to send us something special or if we had visitors coming to Kenya. We always had our eyes peeled for clothing items for ourselves and Kenyans. We typically traced our workers feet on a piece of paper and brought them back nice leather shoes. Daryl would pick out a suit for Antony. Other items on this list ranged from food items to electronic equipment we just could not get in Kenya. An important item that we could never get enough of was video tapes. (DVD's were not available yet.) Without local TV, we watched those tapes again and again.

Under the 'Thank You Gifts' tab we would put down all the names of family members, church members, friends and people that we would be spending the night with. This was the more difficult section to prepare for, because often we would be purchasing a gift for someone we didn't even know. Mainly we bought the things Kenya was famous for—tea, coffee and carved animals. But as we started becoming more familiar with the things that Americans seemed to like, we started buying woven baskets and purses, leather belts, canes/walking sticks, jewelry and carved boxes. Again, at the one year count-down mark, we would start purchasing these items so it wouldn't be so much to buy all at once.

The 'Stateside Itinerary' section would be laid out in calendar form on one page for the whole three months and also a week at a glance. In that way, we could easily anticipate our next trip and the people we would be staying with. That part of the notebook took the most time and the most amount of coordination because it involved so many people and their schedules. We would start by marking out the allotted time for the furlough, put in the time needed for travel to and from Kenya, time with our families and our supporting churches.

That may sound easy enough, but with our overseeing church in Oklahoma, my family primarily in Louisiana, Daryl's family primarily in Virginia, friends and other churches to report to all in between, it was a lot of area to cover in the time allotted. Thankfully, I liked doing this sort of thing so it wasn't a burden. After I had a rough idea of everyone we needed to see, I got out the maps and atlas and tried to figure out the length of each 'leg' of the trip.

There were always two days on furlough we looked forward to. One of them was when we stayed with my sister, Davan. She would take the kids for the day with explicit instructions to, "Go have a date and don't come home 'til late!"

We did leave our kids with other people for short periods of time while on furlough, but never for the whole day and not simply to have time together as a couple. The other day or actually night that we looked forward to was the one night we stayed in a hotel. Throughout the three months of furlough we spent the majority of that time on the road and living out of suitcases. As kind and as accommodating as everyone was, it was nice to have this one night all to ourselves. We would try to find a hotel with a pool and arrive as early as we could so the kids would have lots of time to swim. We would then find a pizza place and have them deliver it to the room and just relax! All that time spent trying to make your kids (and yourself) be on your best behavior could be very wearing. We started noticing that about ten minutes into a new trip, we would all be irritable with each over. Then about an hour later, we'd all be back to normal. It was just the way we released pent-up stress.

The 'Contact Info" tab was simply that. In the days before Google®, MapQuest® and cell phones, we would need to have an up-to-date list of everyone's addresses and phone numbers so we could give someone a call if we got lost or were delayed for some reason. I would usually try to find the name and number of a contact person in the European county we were visiting, just in case we needed it. I would get those names from other missionaries or from the book, *Where the Saints Meet*, by Mac Lynn. When we left for Kenya in 1987, Mac was one of the ministers at the Ross Road church where we attended in Memphis, TN while we lived there. (This church later supported us by contributing to our work fund.) Mac's book gave the address of the last known location of where the church met, a phone number (if there was one), the name of the minister and a few other facts.

The 'Things to Do' tab was a list of all the things we needed to get done *before* we left on furlough. I would make up a list of 'spring cleaning' activities for Kipsang to do while the house would be empty of people. Things like moving the furniture so he could remove old wax and then reapply several coats of new wax. He'd take down the curtains and take them and the rugs outside and give everything a good shake and airing. The beds and bedspreads would be treated in a similar fashion. The refrigerator, pantry and freezer would be emptied out and thoroughly washed down and dried and then the items returned and organized. Supplies would need to be purchased for their chaik breaks and for any of the activities I came up with to keep them busy for the three months of our absence. Daryl would do something similar with Joseph accept that his jobs stayed pretty much the same, year round, since he worked outside. That portion of the book was more to help Daryl because he had so many different things to keep track of— accounts around town paid off or paid in advance of our leaving, the rent for our house kept current and different things we paid together as a team. He would also leave money with our teammates in case something came up in our absence that we had not anticipated. We also left the team our itinerary in case something came up and they needed to call us.

So as you can see, there was a lot to prepare and organize when furlough time came around. The next time you are around a person on furlough, maybe you will understand a little better why they may seem tense or distracted, they probably are. It's hard to have your feet in two countries at the same time. When you are in one, you are thinking about the other and wonder what's going on in your absence. But even so, furloughs were always needed and helped to reconnect us to our families, friends, churches and culture back home.

As we traveled around on our furloughs, we would try to explain how we lived in Kenya, but for many without a point of reference, it was hard to communicate. Slide show presentations, then later videos and even later still, PowerPoint helped us tremendously to give people a little 'taste of Africa'. One furlough, we were in Oklahoma for their VBS, Vacation Bible School program. The church built a cardboard and hay 'mud hut.' Daryl taught the adults and I taught the kids about Kenya and missions. I welcomed the kids barefoot, wrapped in *kangas* and with a doll strapped to my back.

We also had a 'Kenya Night' where we served Kenyan foods and decorated the fellowship hall with all the gifts we had packed to give to people while on furlough. The elders' wives helped me in the kitchen while Daryl and the elders went around with basins and pitchers helping people wash their hands as is the custom in Kenya. After the night was over, some people said they felt sorry for us if that was what we had to eat. Whereas other people said they were happy for us that we had such great food to eat and they wouldn't worry about us anymore!

I found it interesting that when I decided to write about Kenya (primarily for our kids and families to get a better grasp of time there), the experiences that first came to my mind were from the years in Sotik. Those years were such a struggle for me that I couldn't see the things that God was orchestrating. Once again I learned that by listening to God's prompting to put pen to paper about that time in our lives, *I* was the one that was blessed. Writing has helped me to redeem the time that I spent in Sotik. I always felt a bit embarrassed when someone would introduce me as a 'Kenyan missionary'. So many times I wanted to interrupt them and say, "I'm just a wife and mother that happens to be living in Kenya. I'm not a REAL missionary."

ORIGINAL   (r. 15 (3))
FORM 7   REPUBLIC OF KENYA

                  THE IMMIGRATION ACT
                      (Cap. 172)
                  ──────────   SERIAL NO.
                  ──────────

      DEPENDANT'S PASS 125405
                    File No. R. SS6638

Mr./Mrs./Miss...LAURIE WALL BATES...

of (country of residence) ...KENYA...

is hereby permitted to enter Kenya within six months from the date of issue or in Kenya, and to remain in Kenya subject to the Immigration Regulations.

Nationality ...AMERICAN... Security ...N.D.R...

Relationship to Applicant ...WIFE...

Date of Issue ...3.8.88...

Receipt No. ...149792...

Fee Paid Sh. ...500/...Gratis.

                              for: Principal Immigration Officer.

But now, I'm not embarrassed. I'm awed at the way God used that time in my life to stretch me and grow me in ways that I'm not sure would have happened otherwise. You don't have to go to Africa, or 'go' anywhere for that matter, to be stretched by God. I'm finding that my life back in America has been every bit as much of a stretching and growing process as my time in Kenya was. Returning back to America and finding my place here has been as much of a culture shock to our family as it was when we first went to Kenya. So don't think you have to go far away from home to be of service to God. All He asks for is a person willing to do the things He bids them to, whether it makes sense to them or not.

A good illustration of this is the story of Gideon from the Old Testament found in the book of Judges. Chapters 6 to 8 tell of how Gideon, a simple farmer, was standing in the bottom of a wine press threshing his wheat. Actually he was hiding from his enemies, the Midianites. Then God called him out to be a warrior. Gideon's response was: *'Me, Lord? You think I'm a warrior? But, how could I be?'*

The Lord's response was something like this: *'You go with the strength you have and I'll do the rest.'*

Eventually obeying Him, Gideon led the Israelites to victory over the vast Midian army using only three hundred men, clay pots, trumpets, torches and of course, God's help. Isn't this story a lot like you and me? There we are, minding our own business when seemingly out of the blue; we sense a prodding from God to do something. Usually our first response is like Gideon's, *'Me, Lord? You want ME to do WHAT? I couldn't possibly!'*

And like Gideon, we have the option to give excuses, or to even test God. But also, we should say 'I'll go', like he did and not, NO, like we would probably prefer to say. Even when we see ourselves as a simple person; God sees us as a mighty warrior, in His hands. We need to go with the strength we have, as feeble as it is and let God do the rest. If we do, we will be blessed beyond what we could ever imagine or even dream.

In conclusion, I'd like to share an excerpt from the New Testament with you. I have read this passage to people as a way to impart a blessing to them. This is achieved and made more personal by inserting a name at different points throughout the chosen passage. It seems only fitting that I use it here to bless you. (And don't worry, there is no spitting involved!!) You can do this with just about any passage in the Bible. This just happens to be one of my favorites because I was privileged to read it to Lydia at her baptism when she went to summer camp.

If you have a special passage that gives you comfort, faith, courage or hope, use it in the same way and insert someone's name throughout the reading of it. If a passage gives those things to you, wouldn't it be nice to bless someone else with them, too. Plus, God loves hearing you repeat His words to yourself and to others. May God bless you as you listen and learn the lessons that He is trying to teach you. Be prepared, they may come in ways you don't expect!

LESSON LEARNED

Don't ever, ever think you know better than
God what is best for you. He knows you better
(and loves you more) than you can imagine!

"I pray that Christ will be more and more at home in your heart; _____, living within you as you trust in him. May your roots go down deep into the soil of God's marvelous love; _____, and may you be able to feel and understand, as all God's children should, how long, how wide, how deep, and how high his love really is; _____, and to experience his love for yourself; though it is so great you will never see the end of it or fully know or understand it. And so at last you; _____, will be filled up with God himself. Now glory be to God who by his mighty power at work within us, is able to do far more than we _____, would ever dare to ask or even dream of—infinite beyond our highest prayers, desires, thoughts or hopes. May he be given glory forever and ever."

Ephesians 3:17-21(TLB)

Daryl planting a tree in Joseph's 'garden'
for remembrance sake just before we leave
Sotik to manage Kimbilio House in Karen

SPIT IT OUT
(Questions to consider)

"In my mind's eye, You take my hand. We walk through foreign lands; the foreign lands of life."
Song: Mind's Eye by DC Talk

LAUNDRY WITH A MISSION

1. How would you feel if God called you to something?

2. Would you attempt to do what He asked of you?

3. What do you think would happen if you didn't do it?

DREAMS BECOME REALITY

1. Do you think a survey trip is a good idea or a waste of time and money?

2. How do you think you would react if you were surrounded by a language and a culture not your own?

3. Are you a person that likes to sit back and people-watch or jump in and experience new things?

MOMENTS OF CLARITY

1. How do you think you would feel walking up to a hut for the first time?

2. Have you ever cooked over a wood fire? Explain why.

3. How would you like to haul all the water your household used every day?

THE VILLAGE ELDERS DECIDE

1. If given the chance, would you sleep in a hut?

2. What do you think of a group making a decision for you, instead of deciding for yourself?

3. Do you think it's important to try to maintain your own culture while in the midst of another?

READY OR NOT

1. What things would be "must haves" for you to bring with you to set up a house in another country?

2. Would you want to have people working in your home?

3. How quickly should a person adapt to a new culture?

The Sotik Team -four years after arriving, (l-r) Bates Family,
Vick Family and Rogers Family (We all eventually had 3 children)

DRINKING WATER TAKES HOURS

1. How long have you ever had to go without electricity?

2. Would you go out in the middle of a rainstorm to collect water or just do without?

3. Could you bathe in water the color of weak tea or use the water someone else already bathed in?

CULTURE GOES A LONG WAY

1. What aspects of another culture interest you most?

2. What personality trait or characteristic of yours do you think could be used as another name for you?

3. Could you keep your composure if spat upon?

TEA AND A PURPLE SWEATER

1. How would you feel being showered by gifts from someone who needed it worse than you?

2. If you lived in a culture where crying was not acceptable, could you control yourself?

3. How would you feel if someone had walked miles just to give you a simple gift?

THE DAILY (UN)ROUTINE

1. Have you ever had to work as a team? Explain.

2. Could you cook all your meals from scratch?

3. How do you feel when things don't happen the way you plan for them to?

THE GREEN MAN

1. How would you feel if you only had three dresses and one pair of shoes?

2. Could you give up pants and makeup if you needed to?

3. Do you think it is demeaning to pay a bride price or would you feel treasured?

OUR SECOND FAMILY

1. What things would you do at a lengthy meeting (in a foreign language) to occupy your thoughts?

2. Have you ever had a major faux pas? If so, what?

3. Are you able to laugh about it now?

TAXI, AMBULANCE, HEARSE

1. Would you stop to pick up people needing rides?

2. How would you feel about carrying a dead person or delivering the coffin in your vehicle?

3. Do you think you would have to 'get away' to be able to have a day off?

HEAVEN TO HELL IN 60 SECONDS

1. What's the worst accident you've ever experienced?

2. Who is someone you can depend on (here on Earth) to help you out in a time of trouble?

3. When is a specific time that you knew God was watching out for you?

TRIPS TO THE MARA

1. If you heard lions outside your tent at night, would you sleep in the car or remain in the tent"?

2. What animal or event would you most like to see in a game park or with animals in the wild?

3. How do you think you would react if you were attacked by an animal, either tame or wild?

Maasai Mara Game Park, (The Sand River Gate is
visible in the background to the left of tent).

VISITORS TO KENYA

1. How difficult would it be to be apart from your family?

2. When visiting another country, would you prefer to experience day-to-day or "touristy" activities?

3. Would you try to eat local foods or just stick with foods you are familiar with?

TRIBAL CLASHING

1. What's a scary situation you've experienced?

2. If you had to evacuate and could only pack one bag, what would be some of the things in it and why?

3. Where is the "safe haven" you would flee to?

TRY SOMETHING DIFFERENT

1. When living in another country, would you take your children out with you or keep them sheltered at home?

2. If you were unhappy, would you stay where you are or would you try to find something different to do?

3. If you did do something different, would you feel like a failure because you didn't "gut it out"?

HAVING FEET IN TWO COUNTRIES

1. What is something you did, even though you didn't really want to, but later saw the blessing in doing it?

2. Have you ever stopped to think about the chain of events that led you to where you are today?

3. What are some other passages you could use to bless someone, by reading them out loud with them?

Lydia (3 years old) and Steven (1 year old) in
front of a windmill in Brussels, Belgium They are
eating Granny Smith apples for the first time

QUOTE CITATION

Movies

Baby Boom, Dir. Charles Shyer, Perf. Diane Keaton, Harold Ramis, Sam Shepard, United Artist, 1987

Big Fish, Dir. Tim Burton, Perf. Ewan McGregor, Albert Finney, Jessica Lange, Columbia Pictures, 2003

Fiddler on the Roof, Dir. Norman Jewison, Perf. Chaim Topol, Norma Crane, Leonard Frey, Molly Picon, United Artists, 1971

Forrest Gump, Dir. Robert Zemeckis, Perf. Tom Hanks, Robin Wright Penn, Gary Sinise, Sally Field, Paramount, 1994

Lord of the Rings: Fellowship of the Rings, Dir. Peter Jackson, Perf. Elijah Wood, Ian McKellan, Viggo Mortenson, Sean Astin, New Line Cinema, 2001

My Big Fat Greek Wedding, Dir. Joel Zwick, Perf. Nia Vardalos, John Corbett, Lainie Kazan, IFC Films Playtone, 2002

Out of Africa, Dir. Sydney Pollack, Perf. Robert Redford, Meryl Streep, Klaus Maria Brandauer, Universal Pictures, 1985

Secondhand Lions, Dir. Tim McCanlies, Perf. Michael Caine, Robert Duvall, Haley Joel Osment, New Line Cinema, 2003

Tombstone, Dir. George P. Cosmatos, Perf. Kurt Russell, Val Kilmer, Sam Elliott, Hollywood Pictures, 1993

Twelve Angry Men, Dir. Sidney Lumet, Perf. Peter Fonda, Lee J. Cobb, E. G. Marshall, United Artist, 1957

The Wizard of Oz, Dir. Victor Fleming, Perf. Judy Garland, Frank Morgan, Ray Bolger, Metro-Goldwyn Mayer, 1939

Songs

"Blest Be the Tie That Binds," John Fawcett, (Hymn) 1782

"Breath Of Heaven (Mary's Song)," <u>Home For Christmas</u>, Amy Grant and Chris Eaton, A&M Records, Word Records, 1992

"Can You Count the Stars?" (German Folk Tune) Johann Hey, 1921

"Carol's Theme", (<u>The Carol Burnett Show</u>), Joe Hamilton, 1967

"I Will Listen," <u>Where I Stand</u>, Twila Paris, Sparrow, 1996

"Mind's Eye," <u>Jesus Freak</u>, DC Talk, Forefront, 1995

"What Have We Become?" <u>Jesus Freak</u>, DC Talk, Forefront, 1995

"Who God Is Gonna Use," <u>The World As Best As I Remember It, Vol. 1</u>, Rich Mullins, Reunion Records, 1993

"You'll Be In My Heart," <u>Walt Disney Records</u>, Phil Collins, 1999

Books

Kangas:101 Uses, Jeannette Hanby and David Bygott, 1984

Kipsigis Grammar Lessons, World Gospel Mission, Edited by Mary Adkins, 1985

Where The Saints Meet, Firm Foundation Publishing House, Mac Lynn, 1983

Internet

Wikipedia, The Free Encyclopedia, Wikimedia Foundation, Inc, 2004

ABOUT THE AUTHOR

Laurie Wall Bates grew up outside of the city of Thibodaux, a Cajun French area of southern Louisiana. She feels growing up in that diverse culture helped to better prepare her for Africa and missions. Laurie met her husband, Daryl, at Harding University in Searcy, AR. During their last semester, they joined a team that went to East Africa. After almost six years in Sotik, Kenya, they moved to Nairobi, Kenya where they spent an additional six years. All three of their children, Lydia, Steven and  Lee were born at Kijabe Medical Centre, an American mission hospital located in the Great Rift Valley of Kenya.

Upon returning to the States, questions from her children, family and friends about their time in Africa prompted the writing of Spit A Blessing, *Remembrances of Kenya—The Sotik Years*, which focuses on their years spent in the rural areas of Kenya. If you liked this book, you're sure to enjoy her next book under the working title of, Giraffe At Breakfast, *Remembrances of Kenya—The Nairobi Years*. That book will be a continuation of their years spent in Africa, focusing on the time they lived in the international city of Nairobi and the adjustments made between rural and city living.

Kot Kituiyo Kogeny—until we meet again!

The greatest single cause of atheism in the world today
Is christians, who acknowledge Jesus with their lips;
Then walk out the door and deny him by their lifestyle.
That is what an unbelieving world, simply finds unbelievable.

Song: <u>What Have We Become?</u> By DC Talk